# THE INSIDER GUIDE TO

# EASY CAR BUYING

## FIND THE BEST PLACE FOR THE BEST DEAL

**Tony Willard**

# MOTORBOOKS
INTERNATIONAL

First published in 2003 by Motorbooks International, an imprint of
MBI Publishing Company, Galtier Plaza, Suite 200, 380 Jackson Street, St. Paul, MN
55101-3885 USA

Motorbooks International titles are also available at discounts in bulk quantity for
industrial or sales-promotional use. For details write to Special Sales Manager at
Motorbooks International Wholesalers & Distributors, Galtier Plaza, Suite 200, 380
Jackson Street, St. Paul, MN 55101-3885 USA.

Talk to the publisher about this book:
rob@motorbooksinternational.co.uk

ISBN 0-7603-1626-0

Printed in China

# CONTENTS

# FOREWORD

**This book is the most comprehensive aid to car buying ever published in the UK. It is the first to provide a detailed assessment of the 10 ways of purchasing a new or used car, and gives an insight into the methods employed by those selling them.**

The intention is to stimulate all car buyers to investigate ways of getting a better deal, and to encourage manufacturers, franchised dealers and others to do more to meet the demands of consumers.

In the 1980s and '90s, Britain became known as 'treasure island', a market where car manufacturers could get away with charging substantially more than elsewhere in Europe. That is gradually changing: manufacturers are being forced to reduce prices in Britain, improve equipment levels and to lengthen warranties.

As we explain, this has come about through pressure from buyers, intense competition among manufacturers and increasingly efficient production processes. It is though only the beginning: consumer power will keep raising standards in the industry and trade, and ensure keen price competition.

The co-operation of those working in the car business who provided insights into aspects of how manufacturers and dealers work is appreciated. There are many industry professionals who, in private, acknowledge that more must be done to provide a fairer deal for consumers.

But the inefficiencies of the motor industry, and the way manufacturers force sales, are obscured behind clever marketing programmes. The intention of this book (and the motivation of those who assisted during research) is to close the information gap between seller and purchaser.

For most people, a car accounts for a larger proportion of their income than anything other than their home. Cars can give great pleasure to their owners, or expensive heartache. The joy of a first drive in a cabriolet with the hood down takes some beating but even the most minor fault on the car creates anger: owners become ever more demanding.

The core message of the insider's guide is that buyers don't realise they are invariably in a stronger position than those who are selling. The book provides information and contact sources to allow you to increase your knowledge, grow in confidence and control the buying process.

Lists, tables and other information will assist you and the sources are acknowledged. Most notably, Car and Parker's used & new car Chooser magazines provide valuable assessments of cars on your shortlist.

Car's 'the good, the bad, the ugly' feature is noted for the incisive comments on new cars by its experienced road testers.

Parker's used & new car Chooser gives a measured assessment of what people can expect from used models.

The two final chapters provide alphabetical lists of assessments by the magazines.

Now it's over to you to find the method of buying that suits you best, and the particular car that will become part of your life.


Good luck.

Tony Willard

## Introduction

# The grand plan

Devise a strategy to beat an industry
determined to make the highest profit

"In the motor trade people say knowledge is money: now it is
your turn to prove it is true"

**As someone about to buy a car, there are 10 different routes you
can choose. Ignorance of even one of them means you can end up
paying much more than you need. If you fail to understand all the
routes on offer, or head in the wrong direction, your ignorance can
cost you a heap of money. This book explains the potential prizes
and pitfalls whichever way you go, and tells you what really goes
on within the business. It is written by an insider, the former
editor of the retail motor industry's leading trade newspaper.**

On the cover, we offer to save you a 'grand' when you spend a tenner. You can recoup
the price of this book just by asking the company or person selling you a car to fill up
the fuel tank as part of the deal. You can do much better than that though. Trimming
£100 off is simple with insider knowledge. But we're more interested in a saving of
more than £1,000, which can be achieved once you have seen how the motor trade
works.

The present system is geared to sell millions of cars using a scattergun strategy.
You are the sharpshooter who can choose where and when to pull the trigger. It
wasn't your idea that the motor industry should conduct itself in such a convoluted
way, and you need have no hesitation in pushing for the best deal going. You can be
sure the industry will.

A substantial saving requires knowledge, which we explain how to acquire, together
with planning, perseverance and patience. You do not need to love cars to be a winner
in this game. You just need to be determined never again to allow yourself to be
treated as a punter. The very complexity of the way the industry sells its cars gives
consumers a whole range of opportunities to save money.

Car dealers like to say 'the customer is king'. That 'the queen' is often forgotten
betrays the fact that much of the motor trade remains uncomfortably sexist. However,
over the past decade, there have been encouraging improvements in the way the trade

operates, albeit often forced on it by the power of consumers learning to use their muscle. And there are still rogues around, so always be on your guard.

This book provides you with the support to drive away with the best available deal. It is a right we all have as consumers, and the most successful retailers should be those best at pleasing their customers, both at the point of purchase and afterwards.

As this book went to press, the industry was bracing itself for tougher times. It expected to sell 200,000 fewer new cars in 2003 than in the previous year. No manufacturer wants to lose ground in a sales war which translates into lower prices for buyers. It is still too early for a clear economic pointer to the 2004 market, but continuing hot competition is certain. This is both good and bad news for motorists, as we discuss later.

Here is an uncomfortable thought to keep in the front of your mind when tackling the challenge of purchasing a car. Buyer A will pay £7,000 for a car while the cannier buyer B is paying £6,000 for something virtually identical. It happens all the time. Be sure you are not buyer A, the punter. But, in the future, today's bargain can cost you more than the saving, and we will explain that, too.

For there are hazards on the way to finding the type and model you want and need, and the particular car that is right for you. It might be new or used, bought or leased, spotted on your local dealership forecourt or delivered to your door like an expensive pint of milk from a sales centre hundreds of miles away.

News-stands are packed with 'how to buy a car' guides because the ways to acquire a car are infinitely more varied than even five years ago. They offer helpful advice, and some will guide you on the value of used cars, but most share a common flaw: they are written from the outside, looking in. We, from the inside, will advise you which are the best, and why.

Consumers have cottoned on to the abundance of information to be found by surfing the net from home computers. That, though, is merely the first step. We will explain how to play one potential way of buying off against another to extract a lower price. We will cut through the sales patter to reveal how people in the trade are thinking and we will weigh up the risk factor in taking different routes, pointing out the tantalising savings that are possible.

In the motor trade, people say 'knowledge is money'. Now it is your turn to prove it is true. Buying a car is, for most, the next biggest financial commitment after a home. But there are important differences. A home will grow in value, unless you are foolish or unlucky. A car will shed value unless you are extremely astute and highly selective in your purchase. From the outset we have to accept that motoring is financially painful and be determined to lessen the hurt.

Deception is more easily practised when selling used cars than it is with used homes. Mileage counters can be wound back, but nothing can change the date when a home was built. The motor trade is a most unusual consumer industry and operates rather like a bazaar. It's fun to barter for a bangle in the Middle East; but haggling over a £5,000 or £10,000 car is rather more serious. You need perfect knowledge of market practice before venturing into a marketplace like this one.

In the hunt for a new car, you can effortlessly move around the websites or buy a magazine to compare engine power outputs, fuel economy, safety devices and equipment packages. Once the choice is made, you want to buy on price, and that is where a new and more daunting level of decision making starts to kick in.

Should you go to your local dealership, possibly 25 years in business and a supporter of local charities? Or hope to save money through buying from its counterpart in the Netherlands? You can get to know the dealer round the corner and have a chat with the technician who services your car. But is it smarter to save a grand or two on your new car by purchasing via the internet? And, if you go that way, how do you feel about spending thousands on a car without sitting behind the wheel? We will show you how to make the decision that is right for you.

Used cars are infinitely varied. They can be a way to enjoy relatively inexpensive motoring, or present you with a bundle of expensive problems. You can save plenty of money, but buying used is trickier than buying factory-fresh. Assembly line robots ensure that each new hatchback is a precise clone of the original computer-originated design (there are few 'Friday afternoon' cars these days). It is unlikely that you will get a chance to compare used cars of exactly identical specification. Even if you could, each is an individual because of age, mileage, the level of skill of previous drivers, and 101 other factors such as the lingering aroma of wet dogs.

So competitive is the UK motor trade that it makes little profit on mass-market cars when they are new. At least there is not much profit to be made from the well-informed customer. But it is relatively easy to bamboozle the ill-prepared into believing that the advertised price is the final price, then 15 minutes later slice 15 per cent off for a more competitive customer. One smartly-dressed and courteous young salesman told an elderly woman he would be sacked if he cut the price of a used Rover 214 because it was 'such a popular car and so cheap'. She bought it (in more ways than one) without getting any advice and for the recommended retail price. The owner of this book would be expected to do better.

We know from the dealer groups that are listed companies (you can buy shares in them, so they have to disclose their figures to the Stock Exchange) that used cars are massively more profitable for the motor trade. This is because they have control over the purchase price, dictate the selling price, and know hour by hour the transaction price of used cars in the marketplace.

It helps to know exactly who you are dealing with, where their stock comes from, what discretion the salesmen have and what their pressure points are.

You might also want to know who is really trying to sell you a car, and that is not always as obvious as it might appear. If you buy a Skoda from a dealership on the motor retail park on the North Bridge in Doncaster, you are about to become a customer of the Royal Bank of Scotland (RBS). Improbable, but true. RBS paid £110 million for Dixon Motors, one of the largest and most successful dealer chains in the country. You won't see Royal Bank of Scotland or RBS over the door. You might not want to do business with a bank. On the other hand knowledge is power and you might sense an offer of cheap finance. Show you mean business by asking which company owns the dealership.

Dixon Motors supplies cars to Jamjarcars, the internet new car sales operation operated by the Direct Line insurance group which delivers cars directly to your door. You can see how the plot is already starting to thicken as you enter the motor trade labyrinth.

Buy a car from Weybridge Automobiles of Cobham, Surrey, or Romans Motor Company of Harrogate, Yorkshire, and you are doing business with Pendragon, the UK's biggest motor dealer group. Your 'local dealer' may thus be a branch of a major company quoted on the Stock Exchange, with dealerships in Germany and the US.

If you buy from Sytner Group, a British dealer group respected in the trade for its professionalism, you deserve to know it is owned by America's UnitedAuto Group which has a network of 120 or so dealerships in the US.

Go online with Autobytel, one of the biggest internet car businesses, and you are trading with a business born in California and owned in the UK by Inchcape, a public company that runs Wadham Kenning, Mann Egerton and the BMW chain of Cooper outlets.

Here's another twist. In your quest to save money, compare a three-year-old BMW 323i in a Cooper's Sunday newspaper advertisement and one on the Autobytel website. The two ads may well be for the same car and you could make your selection from the two prices. Information is power.

The greatest money-saver of all used to be importing your own car from Belgium or other low-cost countries across the Channel, rather than paying inflated UK prices. It was tricky, but worthwhile. The process has become a great deal easier, but the price saving has fallen. Is it still worth doing? UK car dealers think so. Some of them are selling new cars from Holland, and giving the run around to their official suppliers.

Around nine million new and used cars are bought and sold in the UK each year. Each deal is, or should be, completed only after a negotiation on price. Most sellers of both new and used cars will accept an amount lower than first mentioned. Knowing how and where to clinch the very best deal does become easier once you have viewed the motor trade from the inside looking out.

You have taken a first peep inside the car market and we haven't yet mentioned why some car manufacturers like to sell direct, the reality of bidding at an auction or how to spot small-time traders posing as private sellers.

## Chapter 01

# Franchised dealers

They are the benchmark for car buyers –
a logical starting point in the process

"The best salesmen will be amateur but expert psychologists who know how to soften up customers"

Franchised dealers have a contract giving them the right to sell a manufacturer's cars. They are the vital last link between the producer and you, the customer. When you walk into one of their showrooms, and talk to a salesman, you enter an environment where a host of complex business practices are taking place in the background.

In this and the next nine chapters, we will refer to 'salesmen' for simplicity and because the huge majority of the staff handling sales are men. The one you meet may be genuinely helpful or rudely offhand. Either way, he will probably know only part of the business process that makes the dealership tick. The dealer principal (the person owning or managing the dealership, and almost always male) holds the full set of cards and decides on the tactics needed to create the biggest profit for the day, week, month or quarter. He will share as much information as he needs to with the sales force to motivate them into meeting sales targets set by their boss or demanded by the manufacturer.

The motor industry does not operate like a corner shop buying teabags at 40p a pack and selling them for 80p to cover overheads and provide a profit. Life used to be just as simple for dealers. The profit margin was £500, £1,000 or whatever. Nowadays, the new car catching your eye will have a price tag that's almost always negotiable, and represents a dealer profit margin finally worked out from a large batch of variables.

At the heart of all this is a tension between car makers and their dealers. Manufacturers want to keep control of everything, from the design, production and pricing of the smallest widget used in the construction of a car, to the way it is sold. In their heart of hearts, they know they should leave selling to others, but they worry about losing control of the overall process.

It's important to know how the salesman is categorising you because, when you enter a showroom, it is probably for one of the reasons listed below:

- To buy the car you have always dreamed of owning.

  *Trade viewpoint:* enthusiasm for a particular model, and any hint of eagerness to buy without delay, puts a salesman on the scent of clinching a full-price deal.

- In response to a TV commercial that made a particular model seem appealing for whatever reason: whether it is real desirability, or an offer such as a free loan.

  *Trade viewpoint:* manufacturers spend millions building the appeal of their brands and to tempt you into one of their showrooms. The dealer's role is to persuade you to buy. If a car is advertised with 'free insurance', the cost to the manufacturer/dealer is taking some of the money available for negotiation (on a part exchange, for instance) out of the deal. But you know the model is not selling well enough without support, so the deal is there for the taking.

- You want to take advantage of a seemingly irresistible cashback offer.

  *Trade viewpoint:* you would not expect your food supermarket to give you cashback money without a signature on a credit/debit card, so don't expect it from the motor trade. 'Cashback' is a marketing tool to give you a feel-good glow when the manufacturer needs to cut the price to boost sluggish sales.

- You bought your current car at the dealership, appreciated the aftersales service and want another deal.

  *Trade viewpoint:* this is the reason dealers hope you will return. It costs the motor industry far more to win motorists from another make than to retain them. Your brand/dealership loyalty should come at a price. A little extra can be won on the deal if the salesman thinks you are tempted to go to a rival.

- The dealership is close to where you live and, in a hectic world, you are taking the line of least resistance.

  *Trade viewpoint:* you are the dream customer, ready for plucking. You start with the naive assumption that all dealers are the same and that prices are uniform, so you'll be taken for a ride. Read the next nine chapters before deciding to stick with your neighbourhood dealer.

One of the weaknesses in the way the industry works, and therefore a strength for buyers, is that most cars are commodities. There is invariably a rival product that does the job in much the same way. Production lines keep spewing cars into a market that cannot consume them all through genuine sales: that is, bought with the same enthusiasm as you might a Robbie Williams CD or a Caribbean holiday.

Car manufacturers and their dealers work to one of two methods of selling you a car:

- The price is unrealistic and has to be adjusted (the dealer does not expect to sell at the recommended retail price, and so has to find the level in the market where a transaction takes place).
- The price is realistic and reaffirmed (the dealer believes in the price and repeated sales tell him he was correct).

Manufacturers stay in one of these two categories until they are proved wrong. This can be because the tastes of consumers change as makes and models go in and out of fashion. Oversupply or undersupply is also an important influence.

Cars sold in large volumes are broadly in the 'unrealistic price' category and sales have to be pushed by manufacturers. Sales of only a small minority of cars are dictated by people with a strong desire for ownership.

But life is not quite that simple. A particular range or even an individual derivative can be in short supply, while the dealer struggles to sell the L (most basic) version.

So you, and the dealer selling the car, need to be motivated by incentives.

For you, it is the assurance you are getting the car you want, at the right price, and in reasonable time, that will stop you walking out and shopping elsewhere. For the dealer, life is a lot more complicated.

He has to sell the number of new cars agreed with the manufacturer, even when the once best-seller in the range is past its prime, and the dealer over the road is selling a brand new (and he knows a superior) model for a similar price. Good dealers, selling anything from a few hundred new cars a year to many thousands, satisfy the demands of both their suppliers and their customers.

Franchised car dealers' main roles are controlling prices and representing through the look and atmosphere of the showroom the good feeling a particular make of car conveys to a buyer. Manufacturers prefer selling cars through their own network of franchised dealers rather than other channels (as explained in the next few chapters) because they have control over price and the buying environment (something we explore later).

Franchised dealers are the Establishment of motor retailing and confident they will see off the challenge mounted by internet traders, call centre operators, their counterparts across the Channel (some sell to British franchised dealers) and specialist importers of cars from cheaper European countries.

Surveys suggest UK car owners are, in the main, happy with their local dealers, but newcomers will continue to mount a challenge. The franchised dealer is the most accountable of a car manufacturer's 10 channels to market.

They are probably situated on a road often used by customers who can and should call in if they are unhappy with any aspect of the car. The success, or otherwise, of franchised dealers is influenced by word-of-mouth comments in work places, clubs, pubs and school drop-off zones. A dealer's best chance of managing a successful business is to build a relationship of trust with new customers, and then to retain it.

In a perfect world, manufacturers would supply dealers with just enough cars to meet customer demand. The price would keep the buyer, dealer and manufacturer happy. And the customer would get precisely the right car on the agreed day. Supply and demand would be in perfect balance.

The reality is that the manufacturers selling the most cars in Britain achieve that success by creating demand through advertising, finance deals, special editions laden with extras, and a host of other devices. If 'volume is off' (trade talk for sales failing to meet their target), then a manufacturer may offer the dealer 'pack cars' in the form of a batch of 10 or more at a reduced price, but will insist on being paid more quickly than usual.

This gives the dealer a double inducement to push sales. He receives more profit on the car anyway, plus reduced interest payments on borrowings if he can clinch a deal before payment needs to go to the supplier. Buyers can catch salesmen off guard by asking about special deals on 'pack cars', thus demonstrating they have insider knowledge.

Salesmen will always know the trading margin on a new car, that is

## GRAND CONTENDER

## ALFA ROMEO GTV

### NEW CAR SAYS...
**FOR** Slinky styling, V6 engine
**AGAINST** Acute depreciation
**SUM UP** You still would

### USED PARKER'S CHOOSER SAYS...
**FOR** Panache; performance
**AGAINST** There are cheaper choices
**VALUE** Coupe relatively common, early cars fairly affordable; scarcer soft-top Spider quite pricey

the profit to be made for the dealership when the agreed price and trade-in value, if any, are in balance. But they may be unaware of 'pack cars' and other incentives.

Manufacturers put pressure on dealers in a number of ways. They contact customers to evaluate the overall performance of a dealership (how well reception handles phone calls, courtesy and knowledge shown by salesmen, efficiency of the service department and so on). Bonus payments are based on this payments are assessed on overall performance

## GRAND CONTENDER

### BMW 5 SERIES

**NEW CAR SAYS...**
**FOR** Still great
**AGAINST** Dies soon
**SUM UP** Hard to say no

**USED (1996-2003)**
**PARKER'S CHOOSER SAYS...**
**FOR** Understated elegance; engines; driving pleasure
**AGAINST** Little chance of finding a bargain
**VALUE** No cheap ones - £10,000 only buys you the earliest 520i

Manufacturers needing to work hardest at building or retaining their share of the UK market turn to the biggest franchised dealer groups to get them out of trouble. Within the trade, Reg Vardy plc (based in north-east England) and Scotland's Arnold Clark group are respected by their peers as two of the shrewdest operators. In the North-East, the Vardy name has marketing power and many local motorists like the group's sponsorship of Sunderland football club for £1m-plus a year. Elsewhere it uses different names: at Stourbridge, West Midlands, it revived its Trust brand name after acquiring a VW outlet. The name over the door is Trust Volkswagen which made the manufacturer happy. Pendragon, the biggest dealer group in Britain, likes to keep the family names of dealerships it acquires.

These major groups have the financial resources to buy in bulk and the number of outlets and expertise to 'get them out of the door' (dealer talk for selling them quickly). Despite the size of the groups (annual sales of the top five of each are in excess of £1bn), some are run by traditional dealers who started with small businesses and built empires. Sir Peter Vardy is the son of the founder and Arnold Clark set up his company nearly half a century ago. They buy new, nearly new and used cars at the keenest prices, sell to budget-minded customers and strive for the highest profits. Plenty of others running much smaller dealer groups do the same.

Used cars can look remarkably like new ones when they have been fully refurbished and if they have a personal number plate that does not reveal the

and also on a dealer's success in a particular campaign, which might be for 'conquest' sales (winning customers who traded in rival makes of car). Dealers can be claiming money from a single manufacturer on six or seven campaigns at the same time.

These factors represent stress levels within a dealership, so buyers should be sensitive to signals that sales targets may be out of reach. Study dealers' local newspaper ads for batches of cars with identical or similar specifications. And don't be taken in by the sucker line: 'We've lots of these because they are so popular'.

year of first registration. Private motorists can buy one of five types of car from a franchised dealer:

- New (delivery mileage only - a genuine new car)
- Demo (used by staff to demonstrate the model to prospective customers; query a mileage recording of 1,000 or more as staff may have used car for a weekend or longer - grounds for negotiating price)
- 'Special deals' (bought by the dealer under a manufacturer incentive scheme which may be difficult to identify; but can include heavily promoted special editions, often base derivatives with 'extras' included)
- Nearly new (up to 12 months old which might have been previously driven by the manufacturer's staff, but more likely to have been used by a rental company in a short-term deal with the manufacturer. (Potentially a good buy, see chapter 7)
- Used (older than a year and although probably more expensive than elsewhere, should have the backing of the manufacturer's branded approved scheme, and carry the remainder of new-car warranty, or a fresh 12-month cover)

Whichever you choose, dealership staff will say they want to offer you a high level of service as the motor trade is 'a people business' (it's a familiar cliché in the trade). But car buyers are involved with an industry selling something expensive that will, within a year, be worth a lot less. So buyers need lots of reassurance and dealer

## INSIDER GUIDE TO FRANCHISED NETWORKS

In 1993, there were more than 7,000 franchised sales outlets in the UK but the number is steadily declining. Analysts expect the figure to fall to around 4,500 by 2010. Where two brands are sold under one roof, but with separate doors to the showrooms, this is counted as two outlets. At the latest count, Britain has 5,211 franchised retail car sites, of which 4,365 are solus (selling one car brand) and 846 are multi-franchised (selling two or more brands).

### Total sales outlets (on January 1 of each year)

| Year | Outlets | Year | Outlets |
|------|---------|------|---------|
| 1993 | 7,303 | 1998 | 6,471 |
| 1994 | 7,409 | 1999 | 6,244 |
| 1995 | 7,510 | 2000 | 6,139 |
| 1996 | 7,430 | 2001 | 6,032 |
| 1997 | 6,754 | 2002 | 5,989 |

SOURCE: RETAIL MOTOR INDUSTRY FEDERATION

staff require training to convey reassurance. This is to ensure the welcome is right when people walk in and that the deal is done before they walk out.

The best salesmen will be amateur but expert psychologists who know how to soften up customers and then snare them in a deal. Getting people to sit in a car is the important first step. Salesmen who appear to be chatting informally are probably working to a script developed by the manufacturer. 'As you can see, you get a CD player holding six discs mounted in the fascia – that's an important safety factor because you can change disc by pressing a button while driving...' and so on. When it's time for a test drive, the car is likely to have lots of 'bells and whistles' (trade talk for equipment like heated seats, and air conditioning). Always check what is standard on the car you plan to purchase and try to squeeze an extra or two out of the salesman.

For franchised dealers, selling the used cars parked in a row outside is far simpler than juggling the mass of factors that add up to a profitable new car sale. Used cars are normally more profitable for dealers, too, and acquired through trade-ins, from auctions or through manufacturer-backed used cars schemes. The oldest of these is Vauxhall's Network Q, selling all mainstream makes, and keeping the value of cars within the dealer network, while poor trade-in cars go to small used car traders or for auction.

Dealers always hope that used-car buyers will eventually return for another, or for a new car. One of their problems is retaining contact with the owner because service intervals continue to lengthen. They keep owners' and service customers' names on databases though often these are not kept up to date or used effectively. This can lead to mistakes such as letters being sent to people who have died even when their next of kin has informed the dealership. All businesses are vulnerable to mistakes such as these, but car dealers, like estate agents, MPs and journalists, start from a lowly position in terms of public esteem.

The franchised dealership is, for most people, the best starting point in the process of buying a car.

## FRANCHISED DEALERS

How adventurous  ● ● ● ● ● ● ● ● ● ●

Potential saving  ● ● ● ● ● ● ○ ○ ○ ○

### THE GRAND PLAN
This is the most structured sales channel and you need to work hard to make a saving over and above the special deals orchestrated by manufacturers and their dealers. Tactics: contact five dealers and play them off against each other by getting their absolute best price on the car you want.

# INSIDER GUIDE TO THE BIG DEALER GROUPS

The number of franchised dealerships in the UK is declining because manufacturers demand bigger sales territories run by the best operators. Retail power is being consolidated into the 20 biggest dealer groups. The top five have turnovers (total annual sales) of more than £1bn, according to *AM*, the motor industry magazine. Is your local dealership part of one of them? Ask the staff. Some manufacturers own and run networks of dealerships that you might think were operated by a separate retail business.

| Position | Name | Turnover |
|---|---|---|
| 1 | Pendragon plc | £1.815bn |
| 2 | CD Bramall plc | £1.501bn |
| 3 | Reg Vardy plc | £1.268bn |
| 4 | Jardine Motor Group | £1.242bn |
| 5 | Arnold Clark Automobiles Ltd | £1.098bn |
| 6 | Inchcape Retail | £826.9m |
| 7 | Dixon Motors plc | £804.9m |
| 8 | DaimlerChrysler UK Retail | £796.8m |
| 9 | Camden Motor Group Ltd | £781.8m |
| 10 | Lookers plc | £732.3m |
| 11 | Bristol Street Group | £723.5m |
| 12 | Sytner Group plc | £718.9m |
| 13 | Arriva Motor Retailing plc | £687.9m |
| 14 | Robins & Day Ltd (Peugeot UK) | £632.7m |
| 15 | Renault Retail Group | £609.1m |
| 16 | Hartwell plc | £583.9m |
| 17 | Ryland Group plc | £543.6m |
| 18 | Dutton Forshaw Motor Group Ltd | £499.1m |
| 19 | HR Owen plc | £455.7m |
| 20 | European Motor Holdings plc | £420.6m |
| 21 | Greenhous Group Ltd | £353.4m |
| 22 | JCT600 | £290.9m |
| 23 | Marshall Motor Group Ltd | £288.4m |
| 24 | Whitehouse Group Ltd | £287.7m |

| 25 | Perrys | £267.3m |
|----|--------|---------|
| 26 | Caledonia Motor Group | £245.7m |
| 27 | Quartic Motor Group Ltd | £238m |
| 28 | Priory Motor Group | £217m |
| 29 | Benfield Motor Group | £209.1m |
| 30 | Agnew Group | £200m |
| 31 | Reeve Derby | £191.8m |
| 32 | Parks of Hamilton (Holdings) Ltd | £190.4m |
| 33 | Ilkeston Co-op | £186m |
| 34 | Listers of Coventry | £183.6m |
| 35 | John Martin Holdings | £182.4m |
| 36 | Dick Lovett Companies Ltd | £178.5m |
| 37 | Summit Group | £178.3m |
| 38 | Currie Motors | £177.2m |
| 39 | RRG Group | £173m |
| 40 | William Jacks plc | £171.6m |
| 41 | Caffyns plc | £169.9m |
| 42 | Hendy Lennox Group Ltd | £168.8m |
| 43 | Glenvarigill | £166.7m |
| 44 | Peoples Ltd | £164.4m |
| 45 | Citroen UK | £163m |
| 46 | Smith Knight Fay Group | £161.5m |
| 47 | TC Harrison Group Ltd | £157.5m |
| 48 | Helston Garages Group | £152.7m |
| 49 | AFN Ltd | £151m |
| 50 | Eastern Western Motor Group | £144m |
| 51 | City Motor Holdings | £137.9m |
| 52 | Lind Ltd | £133.4m |
| 53 | Harratts Group Ltd | £132.7m |
| 54 | Brooklyn Motors | £131.8m |
| 55 | Macrae & Dick Ltd | £128.7m |
| 56 | Patterson Ford | £126.6m |
| 57 | Fish Brothers | £117.9m |
| 58 | S Jennings Ltd | £114.5m |
| 59 | John Clark Motor Group | £113.7m |
| 60 | Milcars Holdings plc | £109.7m |
| 61 | Mclean & Appleton | £106.4m |
| 62 | Wayside Group Ltd | £103.1m |
| 63 | Pentagon Limited | £102.6m |

| 64 | Beadles Group | £101.6m |
| 65= | Bestodeck Ltd | £100m |
| 65= | CEM Day Ltd | £100m |
| 65= | First Ford | £100m |
| 68 | Robert Smith Group | £99.2m |
| 69 | Lloyd Motors Ltd | £98.6m |
| 70 | Holdcroft Renault | £96.3m |
| 71 | GK Group Ltd | £96m |
| 72 | Sandicliffe Motor Group | £94.9m |
| 73 | Alperton Group Limited | £92.8m |
| 74 | Harwoods Ltd | £91.9m |
| 75 | Lindsay Cars Ltd | £90m |
| 76 | Vospers | £88.9m |
| 77= | Alan Day Motor Group | £88.6m |
| 77= | Glyn Hopkin Ltd | £88.6m |
| 79 | Gordon Lamb Holdings Ltd | £84.9m |
| 80 | Whites Ltd | £84.5m |
| 81 | John Grose | £83.6m |
| 82 | Yeomans Ltd | £83.2m |
| 83 | FG Barnes & Sons Ltd | £82.9m |
| 84 | Walker Farrimond | £82.7m |
| 85 | Springfield Motor Group | £81.3m |
| 86 | Snows Motor Group | £80.5m |
| 87= | Brindley Group | £80.3m |
| 87= | Meteor Group plc | £80.3m |
| 89 | Stoneacre Motor Group | £79.6m |
| 90 | Donnelly Brothers Garages (Dungannon) Ltd | £78.6m |
| 91 | Nidd Vale Motors Ltd | £75.8m |
| 92 | Johnsons Cars Ltd | £75.2m |
| 93 | EMG Ford | £74.9m |
| 94 | McCarthy Motor Holdings | £73.4m |
| 95 | Gates Group Ltd | £72.8m |
| 96 | Norton Way Motors Ltd | £72.5m |
| 97 | Mainland Investments | £72m |
| 98 | Barratts of Canterbury Ltd | £71.9m |
| 99 | Lifestyle Ford | £71.3m |
| 100 | Gilder Holdings | £70.9m |

SOURCE: AM DECEMBER 2002

Chapter 02

# Manufacturers direct

Buyers seem reluctant to take an internet
Journey or accept a VIP offer

"The dealership becomes something akin to the pick-up
point in a department store when you buy a bulky item"

In 2002, two years after its launch, the Vauxhall Internet Price (VIP) programme was responsible for selling just 780 cars out of the company's total of 214,206 new registrations. Vauxhall would not forecast whether VIP would be any more successful in the future.

The performance of Ford Journey, the UK market leader's rival to Vauxhall VIP, remains a mystery because the company will not divulge 'competitively sensitive' sales figures. It claimed 2002 sales were up on the previous year, and predicted a further increase in 2003. The clear message is that for

Ford, the Journey is proving to be a difficult one. Buyers do not seem to be enthused by the manufacturers' propositions, and there are good reasons why.

Vauxhall was the first car maker to venture into cybersales. Like others, it was responding to what seemed like the birth of a brave new world which, as often happens, proved to be a costly myth for many people. Vauxhall's initial approach was simple and clever and caused a minor stir at the London Motor Show in 1999. The manufacturer unveiled some special editions (mainly based on the Corsa and Astra ranges) with 'dot.com' badges stuck on the back and available only via the internet. With this device, the UK's second biggest car seller showed its commitment to a new form of purchasing that young people were predicted to want, and without the need for costly investment. Vauxhall also managed to win useful column inches in newspapers and motoring magazines by creating the impression of being more modern, more in touch, than its rivals.

In horse-racing terms, it was a safe each-way bet. Vauxhall wanted to be cautious because of uncertainty over how quickly internet sales would take off, while offering Web enthusiasts a blue chip service. This was at the time when internet-based 'import specialists' were popping up everywhere.

Manufacturers knew they had to tread carefully because networks of franchised dealers react badly to sales that bypass them. They dislike big fleet deals at heavily discounted prices because they gain no income from them, while the manufacturers insist they invest heavily in their showrooms and workshop facilities.

The concept of internet sales appeals to car manufacturers' love of control. Via their websites, they can be in direct touch with prospective customers, ask them to register and build a database. Viewed another way, manufacturers see sales derived from their websites as a way of soothing dealers who know some stock finds its way more or less directly from assembly lines to car supermarkets.

'Ford Journey is the natural place to select and buy a new Ford car online', says the introduction, which goes against the aims of its dealers who operate their own websites. Ford

## GRAND CONTENDER

## FORD FOCUS

### 👍 NEW CAR SAYS...

**FOR** Looks, handling, engines
**AGAINST** Stingy kit
**SUM UP** Still the one to beat

### 👍 USED PARKER'S CHOOSER SAYS...

**FOR** Bold styling and packaging; handling
**AGAINST** Too radical for some; will soon be as common as the Escort
**VALUE** Priced to appeal to fleet buyers as well as private motorists; used ones getting cheaper – lots of Zetec and LX cars about

claims 50 million hits (visits) on the Journey site but the 'many' satisfied customers between 2000 and 2002 will have been a tiny fraction of those who looked at what was on offer.

The tone on these websites is reassuring for people who have come to be sceptical about dealers. Vauxhall says: 'Your order will be processed by our dedicated team of Vauxhall transaction managers.' There is an invitation to 'build' your own car, selecting colour and trim, adding factory-fitted options and choosing from a range of accessories.

It is hard to see a time when Ford and Vauxhall, the two companies selling the most new cars in the UK, do not offer internet sales. All their models are currently offered online. At present though, the dribble of sales can hardly justify the investment. But the internet is not going away and this method of buying may grow in popularity. The inclination among car makers is to fight to the bitter end and Ford and Vauxhall will be anxious to avoid admitting defeat. So the leading manufacturers may be tempted to offer more enticing prices as the internet route develops, even though such a policy runs the risk of upsetting their dealers.

But would you, should you, use this method now? It is worth exploring if you enjoy using your home computer to make purchases, plan holidays and gain information. But beware if you are a Mac user: some key parts of Ford Journey are not Mac-compatible, a curious failing.

Not all firms in the manufacturers' networks are prepared to be involved, including some Ford and Vauxhall main dealers. Ford dealers make a smaller profit on a Journey transaction than by selling to a customer in the normal way, and the manufacturer sees nothing unfair about this. In effect, the dealer becomes something akin to the pick-up point in a department store when you buy a bulky item such as a washing machine or TV set. The Ford dealership carries out a pre-delivery inspection, attaches number plates and hands over the car to a customer it

**GRAND CONTENDER**

**AUDI** A6

**NEW** CAR SAYS...
**FOR** Solid
**AGAINST** Old
**SUM UP** Consider second-hand only

**USED (1994-97)**
**PARKER'S CHOOSER SAYS...**
**FOR** Safe; solid; sensibly priced for a quality executive car
**AGAINST** Less fun to drive than most rivals
**VALUE** Good ones are not cheap; even early high-milers retain a quality feel

hopes will return for aftersales service.

So step two is to check whether the manufacturer has a dealer participating in its internet-based sales programme within what you regard as a reasonable distance from home or work.

The Ford Journey website promises to supply a featured car through one of its dealers within 10 working days, but the company has been forced to compensate some disappointed customers. The level of compensation is worked out between Ford of Britain's customer service division executive office and the Ford Journey office, an internal arrangement dressed up as an independent assessment.

All methods of buying a car end up as a compromise between the money you save and the hassle, or lack of it, during the process. Finding the saving you expect by dealing with the manufacturers direct can be elusive.

Manufacturer sales websites have enjoyed limited success, even in the US where they have been promoted for longer than in the UK. Internet sites are attractive to independent businesses, probably selling used cars or non-official imports, which do not need to invest in facilities to support the brand, such as test drives. With these sites, the customer is presumed to be sufficiently motivated by the prospective cost savings to be willing to sacrifice other aspects of the retail experience.

Prices and offers keep changing along with the seasons and difficulties experienced by the manufacturers in keeping sales moving. But a customer might discover website and dealership (recommended retail) prices to be identical, with perhaps a little more offered by the manufacturer in a finance package, such as an interest-free loan over three years rather than two.

There is though the comforting knowledge that the site is an extension of a familiar brand. In Ford's case, a company with a large dealer network, and one that used to build cars in Britain, and still does through its Land Rover and Jaguar divisions. Ford Journey underlines the manufacturer's

## MANUFACTURERS DIRECT

**Ford Journey**
**www.fordjourney.com**
**0845 606 8080**
Information on the site is based on winning people over to Ford if they want to buy online by building their confidence. It provides a useful checklist but Mac users will be frustrated as they cannot get information from parts of the website.

**Vauxhall VIP**
**www.vauxhall.co.uk**
Go to the showroom bar on the top line, highlight, and then scroll down to buying-online.
**01582 694 141**
VIP stands for Vauxhall Internet Price. The website enables you to 'build' a car by choosing options. At that point, before placing an order, you must pay a £20 admin charge, refundable on completion.

determination to keep as many sales as possible under its direct or indirect control. So the site creates niggles of worry for bargain hunters by undermining 'unofficial' websites.

'You see a cheap price and your heart beats faster,' it teases. 'Imagine what you could save! Well, before you get too excited, ask what the price includes. Buying on price alone is often a false economy.'

Vauxhall will say only that its internet price is 'generally different' from the recommended retail price due to the streamlined distribution process. So there is not even a pledge for VIP to be lower. Vauxhall has no interest in web browsers and asks for a £20 administration fee when an order is placed, but it is refunded at the time of purchase. In return, the Vauxhall site allows you to create a 'my home page' link where cars you 'build' by clicking on selected colours, equipment items and so on, can be saved. The step after that is to file an order on the final selection.

This process works best when you know what car you want to own and are searching for the best deal. You have to hope you are shopping at a time when the manufacturer is spicing up its website with some special offers. This way of buying is an alternative to surfing the internet for details and then going to a car supermarket.

Toyota and Renault, two of the most ambitious manufacturers in terms of UK sales, do not bother with a direct-sales website. Both have looked at the concept and rejected it. Toyota research suggests private car buyers are happiest buying from franchised dealers as long as they are treated properly and has no plans for sales online. For its posh Lexus division, the online approach is seen as even less appropriate.

Renault is opposed to direct sales to private customers in France, the UK and the rest of the world. It believes the role of its website is to provide information and then direct people to their most convenient dealership.

It might be expected that BMW's MINI, with its chic appeal to young drivers, would make all sorts of offers for buying online. But it also believes in

## GRAND CONTENDER

### BMW 3 SERIES

RX52 SVV

👍 **NEW** CAR SAYS...
**FOR** Best car in segment
**AGAINST** Every man and his dog has one
**SUM UP** Woof woof woof

👎 **USED** (1991-98)
**PARKER'S CHOOSER SAYS...**
**FOR** Image, smooth six-cylinder engines, great to drive
**AGAINST** Not much standard equipment; less exclusive than some rivals
**VALUE** In its twilight years

selling face to face. This is based on the experience of selling the BMW brand successfully, with its dealers fostering a clubby relationship with customers.

Known sales figures suggest private motorists are sceptical about the savings in buying online. They use this method only if the process conveys the prospect of a big saving when some flexibility in choice of make and model kicks in. A manufacturer giving the back-up of its own and its dealers' resources is hardly likely to give much away and car buyers appear to have worked that out.

## ⋯⋯⟩ MANUFACTURERS DIRECT

How adventurous ● ● ● ● ● ● ● ● ● ●
Potential saving ● ● ● ● ● ● ● ● ● ●

### THE GRAND PLAN
Market leaders Ford and Vauxhall continue to test the market by reducing car prices when ordered from their websites. But most manufacturers still shun this approach, believing that buyers prefer to negotiate directly with a dealer.
*Tactics:* quote the savings available on the Ford and Vauxhall websites when asking about other makes.

JD POWER LEAGUE TABLE 2003

Each year, JD Power (an American company) compiles a UK satisfaction survey of cars. This year's was based on interviews with more than 24,000 owners of cars registered between September 2000 and August 2001 (X- and Y-plate). The survey, covering 138 models, was published in *What Car?* Manufacturers are wary of all independent reviews that assess the happiness or otherwise of people who buy their cars, and especially this one. They prepare to put their marketing team into action when successful and make excuses ('unrepresentative', 'too few owners interviewed' etc) when things go badly. The JD Power survey is the best annual independent assessment of cars sold in Britain. It is a valuable reference source for all who buy cars. JD Power's thorough investigation considers reliability, running costs, performance and more.

| Position | Make | Model | Star Rating |
| --- | --- | --- | --- |
| 1 | Honda | Logo | ★ ★ ★ ★ ★ |
| 2 | Toyota | Yaris | ★ ★ ★ ★ ★ |
| 3 | Lexus | IS200 | ★ ★ ★ ★ ★ |
| 4 | Jaguar | XJ Series | ★ ★ ★ ★ ★ |
| 5 | Smart | City Coupe/Cabriolet | ★ ★ ★ ★ ★ |
| 6 | Toyota | Corolla | ★ ★ ★ ★ ★ |
| 7= | Skoda | Octavia | ★ ★ ★ ★ ★ |
| 7= | Toyota | RAV4 | ★ ★ ★ ★ ★ |
| 9 | BMW | 3 Series | ★ ★ ★ ★ |
| 10= | BMW | 5 Series | ★ ★ ★ ★ |
| 10= | Skoda | Fabia | ★ ★ ★ ★ |
| 12 | Subaru | Legacy | ★ ★ ★ ★ |
| 13= | Honda | Civic | ★ ★ ★ ★ |
| 13= | Mazda | 626 | ★ ★ ★ ★ |
| 15 | Toyota | MR2 | ★ ★ ★ ★ |
| 16= | Daihatsu | Sirion | ★ ★ ★ ★ |
| 16= | Toyota | Avensis | ★ ★ ★ ★ |
| 18 | Suzuki | Ignis | ★ ★ ★ ★ |
| 19 | Saab | 9-5 | ★ ★ ★ ★ |
| 20 | Mitsubishi | Galant | ★ ★ ★ ★ |
| 21 | Subaru | Forester | ★ ★ ★ ★ |
| 22 | Mercedes-Benz | E-class | ★ ★ ★ ★ |

| 23= | Honda | Accord | * * * * |
|-----|-------|--------|---------|
| 23= | Hyundai | Elantra | * * * * |
| 25= | Audi | A6 | * * * * |
| 25= | Rover | 75 | * * * * |
| 27= | Mazda | Premacy | * * * * |
| 27= | Volvo | S60 | * * * * |
| 29= | Honda | CR-V | * * * * |
| 29= | Mazda | Demio | * * * * |
| 29= | Mazda | 323 | * * * * |
| 32= | Ford | Focus | * * * * |
| 32= | Honda | HR-V | * * * * |
| 34 | Toyota | Celica | * * * * |
| 35= | Audi | A2 | * * * * |
| 35= | Audi | A4 | * * * * |
| 35= | Jaguar | S-type | * * * * |
| 38= | Ford | Ka | * * * |
| 38= | Nissan | Almera Tino | * * * |
| 38= | Mercedes-Benz | C-class | * * * |
| 41 | Volkswagen | Bora | * * * |
| 42 | Audi | A3 | * * * |
| 43= | Jaguar | X-type | * * * |
| 43= | Mitsubishi | Space Star | * * * |
| 45= | Mercedes-Benz | SLK | * * * |
| 45= | Saab | 9-3 | * * * |
| 45= | Volvo | S80 | * * * |
| 48= | Nissan | Almera | * * * |
| 48= | Vauxhall | Agila | * * * |
| 48= | Volkswagen | Golf | * * * |
| 51 | Nissan | Micra | * * * |
| 52= | Mazda | MX-5 | * * * |
| 52= | Mercedes-Benz | CLK | * * * |
| 52= | Suzuki | Wagon R+ | * * * |
| 52= | Volvo | S40 | * * * |
| 56= | Hyundai | Amica | * * * |
| 56= | Volkswagen | Polo | * * * |
| 58= | Peugeot | 306 | * * * |
| 58= | Vauxhall | Corsa | * * * |
| 60 | Volkswagen | Lupo | * * * |
| 61= | Skoda | Felicia | * * * |

| | | | |
|---|---|---|---|
| 61= | Vauxhall | Astra | ★ ★ ★ |
| 63= | Subaru | Impreza | ★ ★ ★ |
| 63= | Vauxhall | Zafira | ★ ★ ★ |
| 63= | Volkswagen | Passat | ★ ★ ★ |
| 66= | Proton | Wira | ★ ★ ★ |
| 66= | Seat | Leon | ★ ★ ★ |
| 68= | Ford | Fiesta | ★ ★ ★ |
| 68= | Ford | Puma | ★ ★ ★ |
| 68= | Renault | Scenic | ★ ★ ★ |
| 68= | Volvo | V40 | ★ ★ ★ |
| 72 | Citroen | Xantia | ★ ★ ★ |
| 73 | Volvo | V70 | ★ ★ ★ |
| 74= | Audi | TT | ★ ★ ★ |
| 74= | Nissan | Primera | ★ ★ ★ |
| 74= | Suzuki | Swift | ★ ★ ★ |
| 77= | Alfa Romeo | 147 | ★ ★ ★ |
| 77= | Vauxhall | Omega | ★ ★ ★ |
| 79 | Seat | Alhambra | ★ ★ ★ |
| 80= | Citroen | Berlingo | ★ ★ ★ |
| 80= | Ford | Escort | ★ ★ ★ |
| 82= | Renault | Clio | ★ ★ ★ |
| 82= | Renault | Kangoo | ★ ★ ★ |
| 82= | Renault | Megane | ★ ★ ★ |
| 85= | Hyundai | Accent | ★ ★ ★ |
| 85= | Kia | Shuma | ★ ★ ★ |
| 85= | Mitsubishi | Carisma | ★ ★ ★ |
| 85= | Seat | Arosa | ★ ★ ★ |
| 89= | Citroen | Xsara | ★ ★ ★ |
| 89= | Daewoo | Leganza | ★ ★ ★ |
| 89= | Hyundai | Coupe | ★ ★ ★ |
| 92 | Daewoo | Matiz | ★ ★ ★ |
| 93= | Chrysler | PT Cruiser | ★ ★ ★ |
| 93= | Ford | Cougar | ★ ★ ★ |
| 93= | Mercedes-Benz | A-class | ★ ★ ★ |
| 96= | Kia | Carens | ★ ★ ★ |
| 96= | Mitsubishi | Shogun | ★ ★ ★ |
| 96= | Peugeot | 106 | ★ ★ ★ |
| 96= | Rover | 45 | ★ ★ ★ |
| 96= | Volkswagen | Beetle | ★ ★ ★ |

| 101 | Rover | 25 | ★ ★ ★ |
|---|---|---|---|
| 102= | Citroen | Xsara Picasso | ★ ★ ★ |
| 102= | Ford | Mondeo | ★ ★ ★ |
| 104= | Citroen | C5 | ★ ★ |
| 104= | Suzuki | Grand Vitara | ★ ★ |
| 106= | Citroen | Saxo | ★ ★ |
| 106= | Kia | Sedona | ★ ★ |
| 108 | Daewoo | Tacuma | ★ ★ |
| 109= | Hyundai | Trajet | ★ ★ |
| 109= | Peugeot | 206 | ★ ★ |
| 109= | Peugeot | 406 | ★ ★ |
| 109= | Suzuki | Jimny | ★ ★ |
| 113 | Fiat | Multipla | ★ ★ |
| 114 | Seat | Ibiza | ★ ★ |
| 115 | Renault | Laguna | ★ ★ |
| 116 | Nissan | Terrano II | ★ ★ |
| 117= | Chrysler | Neon | ★ ★ |
| 117= | Daewoo | Nubira | ★ ★ |
| 119 | Suzuki | Alto | ★ ★ |
| 120= | Fiat | Seicento | ★ ★ |
| 120= | Vauxhall | Frontera | ★ ★ |
| 122= | Daewoo | Lanos | ★ ★ |
| 122= | Land Rover | Discovery | ★ ★ |
| 124= | Fiat | Brava | ★ ★ |
| 124= | Fiat | Marea | ★ ★ |
| 124= | Mercedes-Benz | M-class | ★ ★ |
| 124= | Vauxhall | Vectra | ★ ★ |
| 128 | Kia | Sportage | ★ ★ |
| 129 | Peugeot | 307 | ★ ★ |
| 130 | Land Rover | Freelander | ★ ★ |
| 131 | Fiat | Bravo | ★ |
| 132= | Fiat | Punto | ★ |
| 132= | Renault | Espace | ★ |
| 134 | Ford | Galaxy | ★ |
| 135 | MG-Rover | MGF | ★ |
| 136 | Alfa Romeo | 156 | ★ |
| 137 | Chrysler | Voyager/Grand Voyager | ★ |
| 138 | Volkswagen | Sharan | ★ |

SOURCE: JD POWER/WHAT CAR?

## Chapter 03

# Car supermarkets

**'Save £1,000s', they cry; you can, but be sure to read the small print and check the specification**

"Car supermarkets are likely to thrive when the economic going gets tough and people start to look around for ways of saving on their motoring costs"

Car supermarket advertisements clamour for your attention with screaming headlines that would not disgrace a tabloid Sunday newspaper. Unlike franchised dealerships, they do nothing to uphold the image created by car manufacturers in costly TV commercials or in newspaper and magazine advertisements.

Car supermarkets are here to stay though and likely to become progressively accepted as a way of buying new, nearly new and used vehicles. People are willing to forsake smart floor tiles and pot plants associated with franchised dealerships if they can make a significant saving. Car supermarkets respond to a natural urge to save cash, offer a wide choice and represent the birth of a two-tier retail structure. They also perform a valuable service for car makers overburdened with stock.

These retail outlets are better described as 'car markets' because they are far more like a street market than a food supermarket. Tesco, Sainsbury's and the rest, with their in-house bakeries, fresh herbs and extensive wine selections, have grown far too grand to be compared with car supermarkets.

Vernon Ford claims to be the granddaddy of the phenomenon in the UK. He started his business in 1959 initially as a minor venture operated from his home in Holmes Chapel, Cheshire. His vision was to sell cars at a heavy discount and often well below main dealer prices. The business began in the year that saw the birth of the original Mini and it was as big a shock to the system as that daringly original little car. In those days, cars were sold in a far more regimented way than today, to a public still rejoicing at the sight of well-stocked shops less than 15 years after the end of World War II.

Vernon Ford, now chairman of Fords of Winsford, heads one of Britain's growing network of car supermarkets stocking hundreds or thousands of cars and selling via call centres as well. He believes the site at Winsford, Cheshire, is the largest of its kind in the UK.

Ford sells far more than just Fords. Like all car supermarkets, it concentrates on popular models from volume manufacturers sold at a lower price than the one on the windscreen in a franchised dealership. A smattering of more expensive cars enriches the interest for shoppers.

The men running these car supermarkets thrive on doing deals and uphold the best traditions of street traders who buy their apples and pears wholesale at 4am. The cars are sourced from whoever is offering the best deal on the day, and the big operators have teams and agents sniffing out low prices throughout Europe.

Unlike franchised dealers shackled to manufacturers, car supermarkets can purchase any make they like, although some official dealers are quietly buying from importers when prices are lower than they would normally pay. The supermarkets buy from failed internet-based companies in mainland Europe, or from

manufacturers happy to turn a blind eye when flagging sales call for a boost in market share.

This means customers can make substantial savings. But they should be careful, because what appears to be a familiar mainstream derivative of a popular car range may in fact be an air conditioning unit (or another item) short of a full UK specification.

If you have been used to buying cars from franchised dealerships, visiting a car supermarket is like doing a weekly food shop at Aldi instead of Waitrose. Aldi, with 5,000 food stores in the UK and worldwide, has fewer lines and staff than supermarket leaders such as Tesco. Waitrose (part of the John Lewis Partnership) locates its stores in more affluent areas and provides quality goods at a higher price.

Car supermarkets, like Aldi (where you have to buy your carrier bags), operate with no frills. You shop there to save money, not to soak up the ambience. Accept that, and be wary of a couple of potential pitfalls, and car supermarkets may be for you. 'Save £1,000s off the UK list price,' is the cry, and you can.

Many of the new cars come from the Netherlands or other EU countries where prices before tax are lower. But buyers in other countries may not get as much equipment on a particular derivative as their counterpart in the UK. Also, the car sold here new with a three-year warranty might be covered by something less if it was sold elsewhere in the EU where car buyers are less demanding. Car supermarkets say they explain this to potential buyers. Sometimes they don't need to.

## GRAND CONTENDER

### DAEWOO MATIZ

S36 LBY

**NEW CAR SAYS...**

**FOR** For Cheap, fun, fizzy 800cc engine
**AGAINST** 'I don't know anything about cars' image
**SUM UP** So cheap it makes sense

**USED PARKER'S CHOOSER SAYS...**

**FOR** Style; space; equipment
**AGAINST** Puny engine
**VALUE** Generous equipment for little money; three-year/60,000-mile warranty; free servicing for first three years

Many streetwise customers expect to pay extra to top up the warranty, and still make a saving on prices at a franchised dealership.

The success of these automotive emporia is dependent on the skills of the buying teams, the systems put into the business and the staff. Sales over the phone are said to be rising because today's young buyers are more likely to buy a new car unseen than were their parents.

Use of the word 'supermarket' does

become appropriate when the products and services in addition to the car are considered. Warranties 'at trade prices', 'outstanding' finance deals and 'instant quote' insurance get headline treatment in the car supermarket ads. You will probably need a magnifying glass for the small print at the bottom of the ad, but be sure to read it all. This reveals, for instance, that the finance package quoted prominently as a weekly payment is based on 6,000 miles a year and that there will be a charge for extra mileage. Do not forget you will also have to pay a deposit up front.

Car supermarket bosses assume customers will have thoroughly researched the websites of manufacturers and those of competitive retailers. You get the chance to sit in the car, which is useful for comparing a handful of competitive models in a couple of hours, but not a test drive. The supermarkets work on the 'stack 'em high' principle, and on a high volume of sales.

Two of the heavy hitters in this sector are Derby-based Motorpoint ('the UK's No 1 car supermarket') and Trade Sales of Slough ('officially the UK's No 1'). Be ready for a sales process with all the subtlety of a heavy metal band. Each company says it has a stock of 4,000 cars or more.

Car supermarkets are likely to thrive when the economic going gets tough and people start to look around for ways of saving on their motoring costs. So in 2003, when the new car market was set to decline compared with the previous year, Motorpoint was opening its third outlet (in Glasgow) and made clear its intention to sell in

# INSIDER DATABASE: CAR SUPERMARKETS

Fords of Winsford
www.fow.co.uk
0845 345 1016

Motorhouse 2000 Ltd,
Cannock, Staffs
www.motorhouse2000ltd.co.
uk
0845 346 777

Motorpoint of Derby
www.motorpoint.co.uk
0870 12 54321

The Great Trade Centre,
White City, London
www.greattradecentre.co.uk
020 8969 5511

Trade Sales of Slough,
Slough, Berks
www.trade-sales.co.uk
08701 220 220

two more areas. It believes five sites are adequate to cover the main population areas of the UK. People are prepared to travel to save a grand or more and, according to Motorpoint, telesales of unseen cars are rising.

Motorpoint, whose annual sales in 2003 were running at around £250 million, has a strong pedigree. One of its directors is David Shelton, the car-buying brain at Motorhouse of Cannock, Staffordshire, which was one of the idiosyncratic nearly new/used car centres bought by the Car Group. That was in 1998, 11 years after it was founded.

Acquisition of cars that are right for the area, and their rapid sale, is at the cornerstone of the way these firms operate, so try to find stock that has been hanging around and go for the jugular on the deal.

Car Group crashed because it believed it could replicate regional sales successes around the country and

tried to force unwanted cars on those living in its catchment area. It was also caught by a disastrous plunge in used car prices and this meant that its ageing stock was losing value.

Prior to the venture into Scotland, Motorpoint claimed a total of 500 sales a week at its Derby and Burnley, Lancashire, sites together with some 120,000 satisfied customers. The Burnley and Glasgow outlets are newly built but HQ is at the jaded Derby centre. One of Motorpoint's rivals is Trade Sales of Slough, not to be confused with The Great Trade Centre ('the UK's greatest car supermarket') at White City, west London, three miles from the site of the new national soccer stadium. The Great Trade Centre claims 'up to 5,000 cars in stock'.

Motorhouse 2000 Ltd ('the UK's premier independent retailer of new and nearly new vehicles') advertises 'European price levels from the heart of the UK'. It is close to the M6 and, like all car supermarkets, near a motorway to make it easy for people living some distance away to get there easily.

Big car supermarkets can be intimidating for the first-time visitor and some people will prefer to pay a visit to get the feel of the operation before starting to look for a purchase. On many sites, a 'meeter and greeter' is positioned to welcome you (they are easy to evade) but sales staff are told to allow people to wander. 'Feel free to browse around... see a sales representative for assistance,' says one of the welcome packs. 'Want to sit in the car? No problem!' it adds. You make a note of the code number on the screen or the registration and visit the key centre. There is no chance for villains to make a speedy getaway because the cars are parked so tightly together.

The biggest savings tend to be on what the trade calls 'run out stock'. These are models rapidly losing their appeal after manufacturers have announced a replacement. They are sold as nearly new (they have probably had a spell on a rental fleet) and it is easy to find them at half the recommended retail price, typically saving anything from £4,000 to £8,000, depending on the model.

You will want to know whether the car you plan to buy has a full UK specification, what warranty remains, who has owned it, the mileage and service history. The big car supermarkets have too many cars to put them all on display simultaneously so it is worth asking what else is available before making a decision.

## GRAND CONTENDER

### DAIHATSU FOURTRAK

**NEW CAR SAYS...**
FOR Farmers love them
AGAINST Farmers love them
SUM UP Farmers love them

**USED PARKER'S CHOOSER SAYS...**
FOR Sturdy; long-lived
AGAINST Poor on-road ride
VALUE Tough, practical, capable and versatile; excellent off-road or for light towing

Car supermarkets tend to employ only male staff because, they say, women dislike the cold. When covered, sales areas usually have an opening to the rest of the stock where the fourth wall would have been.

Women and men work in telesales areas where they need to be motivated by a bonus of as little as £15 a car. That may not sound much, but at one car supermarket 1,400 calls a week converted into 120 sales. By phone, valuations are given on part exchange deals subject to inspection when the owners arrive to collect their next car.

The process of car purchase in the UK is becoming more relaxed and car supermarkets represent the equivalent of fast food outlets. The success of at least some of the pioneers seems assured but, like franchised car dealer groups, the strongest will most probably squeeze out the weakest and acquire the most promising.

 **CAR SUPERMARKETS**

How adventurous  ●●●●●●○○○○

Potential saving  ●●●●●●●●○○

### THE GRAND PLAN
The market atmosphere does not suit everyone, and you are not made to feel special. But there are big potential savings, provided you make sure the car you buy has a full UK specification and warranty. If necessary, buy an additional year's cover.
*Tactics:* check where the car has been before buying.

Chapter 04

# Internet traders

**Offering major savings but still not widely accepted – and Virgin Cars has opened a dealership**

"Buying via the internet, or from a linked call centre, brings the lure of 30 per cent or more off manufacturers' list prices"

Internet traders argued that many people neither liked nor needed car dealers. They claimed customers would be happy to trade online with a company able to cut costs because it had no roof overhead, especially not a showroom. Yet, in one of the more ironic turnarounds in the history of car sales, Virgin Cars, one of the internet pioneers, decided to open a physical dealership in 2003.

The idea of buying a car online began in California, home of Silicone Valley and frontier of the internet revolution. After close to a decade, the process has failed to become the Brave New World of car buying in the US, UK or anywhere else. Doubters who said that for most people the internet was no more than a valuable research medium have so far been proved correct. The pioneers have been forced to rethink in an attempt to stem losses and create viable long-term businesses.

Virgin Cars and the rest have found the going hard but would argue that it's still early days and it took Japanese car manufacturers a long time to become established in Europe. Now Toyota, Nissan and Honda have major European plants in the UK. Maybe, just maybe, the internet will one day become dominant, but it looks unlikely in the foreseeable future.

The internet is most likely to work for people who get a kick from being and buying online. The premier sites have become easy to navigate, even for those who find this an uncomfortable medium. But it's an incomplete method because the internet can take you only to the point of order. The car still has to be collected or delivered.

Internet traders make sense primarily for people who know exactly what they want. This makes price and delivery time the main factors to be negotiated. An internet trader you trust to deliver the goods within an agreed period is as entitled to your order as a franchised dealer or anyone else.

Whether the company is based in the UK or abroad, you will want to know who you are dealing with. So trust plays a major part in this method of buying. People trading online must be certain their money is safe and that they can get answers to their questions and allay concerns. They may tell dark stories about local dealers, but at least they know where they are, and can call in to complain if dissatisfied.

Dealers, forced out of their customary apathy to respond to this expected consumer demand, understood their advantage of being in the buyer's locality. They also tackled the potential market by setting up their own websites. The business jargon for this arrangement is 'bricks and clicks'. The phrase was comforting, convincing many dealers they were part of the new retail thinking. But, in reality, they are only slowly realising that people enquiring online have a mental process that demands rapid responses. All but the most progressive dealers are failing to make a member of staff responsible for online enquiries. The specialist internet traders tend to be

rather better at dealing with online enquiries, as proved by test e-mails during research for this book.

Over the past decade, computers have become almost as part of households as TV sets but used primarily as a means of gaining data and information. The decision to purchase online demands another leap forward. There is a huge difference between meeting a salesman to discuss the purchase of a car and

## GRAND CONTENDER

## CITROEN C5

### NEW CAR SAYS...
**FOR** Big, diesels, equipment
**AGAINST** Ugly, auction-fodder depreciation
**SUM UP** Perfect minicab

### USED PARKER'S CHOOSER SAYS...
**FOR** Space; comfort; 2.0 HDi performance
**AGAINST** Steering and brakes lack feel
**VALUE** Specifications generous; depreciation steep but not that much worse than Primera, 406 and Laguna

## INSIDER GUIDE TO SPOTTING A 'CLOCKED' CAR

- Legal rights enforceable only against a business in existence, so look for an established recommended business for security
- Car must conform to any description it has been given or representation made regarding its condition or history (such as 'reconditioned engine')
- Car must be of 'satisfactory quality and fit for the purpose intended' and meet the standard expected for its description, price, age and mileage
- This requirement cannot be excluded with signs such as 'sold as seen'. Failure to comply is a breach of your rights, for which you may be entitled to compensation or your money back.
- Terms of warranty/mechanical breakdown insurance agreements vary but usually exclude 'wear and tear. They may also have a limit on the amount of each claim. It is essential to check terms you are entitled to.
- The rights detailed above are independent of each other. If you are not covered under one heading, try another.

SOURCE: RAC

clicking your way round a website. Recognition of an internet retailer's brand name, and what it stands for, is crucial because, after the initial search, you will agree terms by phone. The brand issue is the biggest plus factor for Virgin Cars. The others have to invest in building an image and a recognised name, not just in the processes that make the business work. Then there is the big question of where internet traders get their cars.

Virgin's main rivals, Jamjarcars and Autobytel, both have links with franchised dealer networks. After three years operating online and by phone, Virgin decided it also needed its own dealership. This was a new way of thinking. It was the birth of 'clicks plus bricks'.

Buying via the internet, or from a linked call centre, brings the lure of 30 per cent or more off manufacturers' list prices, and it's a channel that can work for those prepared to buy a car in stock. Place an order for something that isn't, and you face frustrating delays because manufacturers give priority to their dealers.

In theory, that gives Jamjarcars and Autobytel an advantage over Virgin Cars. Jamjarcars is a division of Direct Line which established itself in the car market through insurance and has branched into loans, breakdown cover and now car sales.

Jamjarcars buys its cars from Yorkshire-based Dixon Motors, one of the biggest car dealer groups in the UK. Founder Paul Dixon and his staff will sell you a car from one of his dealerships, complete with face-to-face service, or via Jamjar. He makes money either way and higher sales volumes

## INSIDER SIX-POINT TRADING CHECK

- Be convinced you are dealing with a substantial company that has financial resources and a sound reputation.
- Obtain a copy of its conditions of sale, probably available on a website.
- Check on the deposit required and be sure it will be returned if the car you ordered, complete with specified equipment, is not delivered within the period of time you have agreed.
- Get the name of the company supplying the car. If the trader says it might be one of several, insist on all of them.
- Establish a contact point so that you can check regularly on whether the stated delivery date will be honoured.
- If you become suspicious, tell the company you are writing to them (get the name of the managing director) and send a copy to your local trading standards office.

give a dealer greater clout in negotiations with manufacturers.

Autobytel (automobile by telephone) was founded in 1995 and recorded a small first profit in the final quarter of 2002 but, in the year as a whole, lost around £13 million on a turnover of around £50 million. That turnover (of the world's biggest internet car trader) would have been too small to get a UK car dealer group into the top 100 judged on annual sales.

Autobytel has spent a fortune trying to get its name established. The company spread from America to other key markets including Japan and Australia, as well as Europe. It sold its UK business (started in 1998) to Inchcape Group which runs global car distribution operations and has a franchised dealer group called Inchcape Retail in the UK. In effect, Autobytel is to Inchcape Retail, as Jamjarcars is to Dixon Motors. Autobytel and Jamjarcars say they source all cars from the UK. In other words, they are supplied by UK plants or through supply chains operated directly or indirectly by manufacturers.

Virgin Cars, founded in May 2000, spreads its net wider in the acquisition of stock with many cars sourced in Continental Europe. The country of origin does not matter to customers because all have UK specifications.

Over its first three years, Virgin Cars evolved in a way that Sir Richard Branson, Virgin Group chairman, never expected. And in a more costly way than he forecast, too, because Virgin had to inject additional cash into the venture. On launch day, Sir Richard (always a man with an eye for creating a headline to boost his group's image) forecast that Virgin would become Britain's biggest car retailing group. Dealer bosses wished him well because they were certain it would never happen.

Based on Virgin Cars' experience, internet car traders are savvy, middle-aged buyers who know the car they want, and demand a healthy discount with delivery on time. Virgin Cars has steadfastly claimed that choice and convenience, rather than purely saving money, are the factors attracting their customers.

The problem has been that those customers are often professionals with communication skills enabling them to make a fuss effectively if delivery is delayed. This vocal minority forced Virgin Cars to introduce a 'no quibble' deposit-back guarantee if a delivery was delayed by more than 20 working days, in effect a month. It was a way of reducing the time and cost of employing staff to placate disappointed customers. Though welcome, the move goes only some way to allaying the disappointment of a delayed delivery.

Virgin Cars blames the delays and cancelled orders on manufacturers for giving priority to their dealers because they are the 'acceptable face' of the brand (at least when it suits them; networks have been culled ruthlessly over the past decade).

In the late 1990s, car buyers were expected by some to switch in droves from dealerships and other established ways of buying to the internet and call centres. But people turned out to be remarkably resistant to the lure of lower prices and a wide choice. Running a hand over a car's upholstery at the showroom round the corner, and shaking a hand, remains a compelling ingredient in the car-buying experience.

The need for trust is at the root of the internet/call centre car business. People are gradually getting accustomed to buying books and DVDs over the internet, and will book concert seats and holidays by credit card. A car is different because of the amount of money involved and all the problems that might crop up later. The trump card for Virgin Cars is the Virgin

brand. People are used to buying CDs from the group's stores and may even have one of its pensions.

In the 1990s, internet-based sales operations grew rapidly, set up with little capital and holding out the promise of cheap cars from across the Channel. Car manufacturers were dismayed at the prospect of an unruly market, but were hampered in the way they responded by the need to observe EU competition rules.

The call centre market mushroomed during the ill-fated

## GRAND CONTENDER

### ROVER 75

**NEW CAR SAYS...**
**FOR** Residual Honda reliability
**AGAINST** Ancient, creaky, overpriced
**SUM UP** Totally outclassed

**USED PARKER'S CHOOSER SAYS...**
**FOR** Rover refinement and heritage; elegant Tourer estate
**AGAINST** Mid-range Audi, BMW and Merc models
**VALUE** Standard equipment is generous; attractive as a used choice

# INSIDER INTERNET CAR TRADER DATABASE

**Autobytel**
www.autobytel.co.uk
0800 783 1514

**Broker4Cars**
www.broker4cars.co.uk
01773 512 806

**Carseekers**
www.carseekers.co.uk
01506 505 115

**Jamjarcars**
www.jamjar.com
New 0845 644 3524
Used 0845 644 3525
Lease 0845 128 5130

**Showroom4Cars**
www.showroom4cars.com
0870 753 4444

**Virgin Cars**
www.virgin.com/cars
Enquiries: 0845 270 2277

**Woodard Motor Solutions**
www.wmcars.com
01435 813 516

**Wundercars**
www.wundercars.com
01904 693 456

'internet revolution' that saw fortunes staked and lost, but then entrepreneurs started to experience niggling delays that upset customers. Manufacturers became more awkward and sought to keep control of distribution and sales. They are often critical of their franchised dealers, but prefer a defined system to a free-for-all.

In the autumn of 2002, Virgin, the renegade car seller, and a manufacturer signed a remarkable agreement. MG Rover said it would supply cars directly to Virgin Cars and so bypass the franchised dealers who had loyally stuck with the manufacturer during its struggle to survive. The move was bitterly resented by dealers (see also chapter 15 - 'An ever-changing industry').

Virgin Cars has been the most innovative internet trader and tried to maximise the use of its corporate brand. But car manufacturers become uncomfortable when a retailer appears to be overstepping itself and the opening of a sales point at Salford Quays, Greater Manchester, is as significant as the deal with MG Rover. The site was previously used by Reg Vardy plc (one of the big three dealer groups) as part of its Motor Zone used car sales network.

If the Salford Quays experiment is a success (and Virgin Cars makes no such assumption) there could be four or five others around the country in major population areas. Manufacturers will be sensitive to the way cars are sold and displayed, and to rivals getting preferential treatment. Car buyers would surely like a sales point where popular models are grouped for comparison but the producers hate the idea of expensively created brand images being blurred.

Virgin Cars has a link with a franchised dealer group. Its disposal/collection point at Leighton Buzzard, Beds, is part of a 15-acre

## INSIDER GUIDE TO CARS YOU MUST DRIVE

We all have our preferences but there are 50 cars we should all drive before we die, according to a panel of motoring experts. Many using this book to help them spend less on their next car will have driven a version of the No 1 car: the original Cooper Mini. The choice of No 36 suggests the panel had a sense of humour.

1 Mini Cooper (original)
2 McLaren F1
3 Porsche 911 C2
4 Ford Model T
5 Citroen DS
6 Ferrari 575 Maranello
7 Lamborghini Murcielago
8 Jaguar E-Type
9 Lotus Elise Mk 1
10 AC Cobra
11 Bentley
12 Caterham 7
13 Volkswagen Golf GTI
14 Subaru Impreza Turbo
15 Fiat 500
16 Volkswagen Beetle
17 Citroen 2CV
18 Peugeot 205 GTI
19 Mercedes S55
20 Range Rover (new)
21 Dodge Charger
22 Ford GT40
23 Mercedes Pagoda SL
24 Land Rover Series 1
25 Audi Quattro
26 Honda NSX Type R
27 Aston Martin Vantage
28 Ford Escort Mexico

29 TVR Tuscan
30 Range Rover (original)
31 LTI Taxi
32 MINI (new model)
33 Austin 7
34 Smart Cabriolet
35 Ford Sierra Cosworth
36 Austin Allegro
37 Alfa Romeo V6
38 Saab 92
39 Datsun 100A Cherry
40 Morgan
41 DAF55
42 Nissan Skyline GT-R
43 Nasty £5 nail *
44 Jaguar XJ
45 MGB
46 Morris Minor
47 BMW Z1
48 Suzuki Cappuccino
49 Toyota Prius
50 Sinclair C5

* This is described as 'the last unwanted car at an auction, such as an ageing Citroen XM or a Ford Granada'.

SOURCE: AUTO EXPRESS

preparation area operated by Camden Motors, a large franchised dealer group, which checks and stores cars for the internet trader.

Customers who want delivery to their door are charged £230 by Virgin Cars and this is why an increasing number of customers buy one-way train or coach tickets and collect.

Virgin Cars claims now to supply 85 per cent of cars early or on time and says it is becoming easier to get stock as manufacturers come to accept the company as an established provider of its brand.

Virgin Cars, Autobytel and Jamjarcars could be paving the way for a transformation of the way cars are sold in the UK. Or, say continuing sceptics, they will turn out to be no more than a footnote in the history of the way cars were sold.

Even if one or more of these companies failed, the risk for customers is minimal. There is no suggestion that Sir Richard Branson plans to put Virgin Cars down to experience and give up, although he must wonder how and when his group's investment will see payback time. The success or otherwise of the Virgin Cars sales outlet in Manchester holds the key to the future of the business.

···>  **INTERNET TRADERS**

How adventurous  ●●●●●●●○○○

Potential saving  ●●●●●●●●○○

**THE GRAND PLAN**
Prices are listed and offer big savings, but the adventurous part is the continuing uncertainty over delivery times. The decision by Virgin Cars to open a dealership indicates that internet sales have not caught on well.
*Tactics:* it is essential to establish a line of communication so that you can chase your order.

## Chapter 05

# Importers

## You could easily save a grand but you need to be adventurous and to watch the detail closely

"Importers relish raising two fingers to officialdom and so do their customers"

Deciding to buy an import takes the purchaser outside the distribution structure created by the manufacturer. There is nothing illegal about it, and you could easily save more than the grand we are aiming for, but being a rebel involves risks. This method is for the more adventurous and the better informed.

Importers can be bracketed with the internet traders examined in chapter 4. They rely heavily on websites as a convenient way of offering their goods and car buyers attracted by this route tend to be comfortable with electronic research.

Essex-based Broadspeed operates at the point where internet traders and importers merge. Simon Empson, the founder, was among the importer pioneers and in 1998 started 'car-buying cruises' to Holland. Broadspeed staff looked after the paperwork on the way out and customers caught a ferry back with their new car.

Broadspeed says it placed orders for 22,000 cars with Continental dealers between 1998 and early 2003 when it also began dealing in UK-sourced, discounted cars as reports circulated about a glut of stock caused by reduced demand. According to Broadspeed, three out of four people making enquiries would prefer their car to come from a company in the UK, suggesting a continuing unease over imports among many car buyers.

Broadspeed, praised by *Webuser* magazine for a website (www.broadspeed.com) 'simply miles ahead of the opposition', charges a fixed fee of £150 on each car paid for and delivered. Step one with importers is establishing how much they intend to charge and at what point in the transaction.

'Importers' is a convenient name to differentiate between these traders and the 'official' distributors of cars built in the UK or another country. No law says cars must be imported into Britain in a particular way, but there are taxes to be paid and various rules to be observed over issues including safety. The importers relish raising two fingers to officialdom and so do their customers.

They are more properly called 'parallel importers' because their supply stream from mainland Europe runs alongside the official one controlled by the manufacturer. These importers are sometimes also exporters because a number of companies have been set up in Holland, Belgium and other European countries to supply dealers and private buyers in the UK. This rather cumbersome state of affairs came about because Britain and other EU countries have different rates of tax on new cars. It is why Jaguars, Range Rovers and other cars built in Britain are cheaper when imported into the country. Manufacturers in Britain or abroad move cars from assembly lines to ports and hold them at points in the UK before distributing them to dealers, fleets and sometimes car supermarkets and other retailers.

Some overseas manufacturers

GRAND CONTENDER

## BMW 7 SERIES

**NEW CAR SAYS...**
**FOR** Clever
**AGAINST** Too clever by half
**SUM UP** Cyborg killer limo, feels neither pity nor remorse

**USED** (1994-2002)
**PARKER'S CHOOSER SAYS...**
**FOR** Performance; refinement
**AGAINST** Running costs
**VALUE** Getting on a bit and just replaced, but a superb used car for the money

have always owned their UK distribution arms and, over the past decade, most of the others have followed suit. It is part of the manufacturers' desire to have total control over production, preparation of imports prior to distribution, prices and costs.

A true parallel import will have precisely the same equipment specification as a corresponding car sold by a UK franchised dealer. And it will be right-hand drive, of course. These cars are not the same as so-called grey imports with equipment levels appropriate to their country of

## GRAND CONTENDER

## FORD FIESTA

### 👍 NEW CAR SAYS...

**FOR** Space, dynamic prowess
**AGAINST** Lacks surprise or delight
**SUM UP** Brilliant to drive, otherwise feels cheap

### 👍 USED (1995-99)
### PARKER'S CHOOSER SAYS...

**FOR** Lively 16-valve engines; much improved ride and refinement
**AGAINST** Not enough room for rear passengers or luggage
**VALUE** Used prices have tumbled because of high volumes; Encore models have miserly equipment.

origin, but not necessarily the same as the corresponding model sold in the UK. Some used grey imports come from Japan. One of the most popular has been the Eunos roadster, sold here as the Mazda MX-5. The Eunos is naturally right-hand drive because Japan also drives on the left. Grey imports from Japan are mainly high-performance sports cars or saloons.

Some internet traders (such as Autobytel) trade closest to the manufacturers' preferred way of operating because they deal only in UK-sourced cars. These will be built in the UK and acquired from the official distributor, or one of its customers such as a dealer or rental fleet operator.

In the 1990s, importers sprang up because new cars in the UK were generally much more expensive than in other European countries. There were two main reasons:

- Manufacturers charged higher prices in Britain than elsewhere in the EU and got away with it for decades.
- Varying tax levels within Europe meant there was, and still is, a price advantage for Britons who buy cars supplied in another EU country.

Cars in the UK carry a basic price set by the manufacturer to which 17.5 per cent VAT is added and then passed to the Exchequer. In other European countries, taxes are generally higher and manufacturers have to fix a lower base price, otherwise cars would be ludicrously expensive. Holland, for example, has a double tax system in place on new cars and this adds, on average, 52 per cent to the base price. Denmark and Greece also have high car taxes.

Holland became the main source of UK imports because it also has convenient ferry routes from the Hook of Holland and Rotterdam. Another advantage is that most Dutch people speak good or even perfect English.

VAT is automatically added to the price of a new car bought in the UK and must be paid when an imported vehicle arrives in the country. When Renault exports a Clio from France, it is responsible for obtaining the necessary clearance from Customs & Excise, completing forms and paying the appropriate taxes. For manufacturers, this is a routine procedure. For you, it is probably more daunting. You can pay more and still save money by going to an importer, or Continental exporter, who will look after the bureaucracy.

Importers in the UK began as a band of buccaneers who seized a market opportunity. At first, manufacturers frowned on them but took little notice, regarding the traders with as much concern as a restaurant owner who notices a caravan burger bar with Union Jack flying in a lay-by a mile down the road.

But the importers became better organised, bolder and more professional. They started to take significant chunks of business away from franchised dealers and grouped together in the British Independent Motor Trade Association (BIMTA). They remain on the fringe, tolerated by manufacturers forced to uphold EU competition laws. But the impact of the importers was sufficient to force a number of manufacturers, including Mercedes-Benz, to cut prices. The more expensive the car, of course, the bigger the potential saving.

To be successful using this channel, you need to be wary, work with established traders and take care to avoid potential villains. BIMTA has a code of conduct that, in its words, 'gives you a chance of some sort of comeback if things go badly'.

Largely, though, it's down to you. Most of the rules when operating outside formal procedures come down to common sense, and to retaining a sense of caution. Always, for instance, get a detailed specification of a car you are buying and compare it with the model sold in the UK. It is worth asking at your local franchised dealership for a specification sheet because, if salesmen are on their toes, they will try to persuade you to buy from them instead. This could be a way into a deal that possibly costs you less than if you had called there first, but more than agreeing to buy from an importer. It

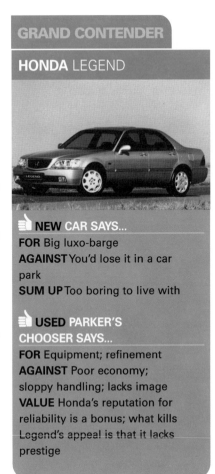

## GRAND CONTENDER

### HONDA LEGEND

**NEW CAR SAYS...**
**FOR** Big luxo-barge
**AGAINST** You'd lose it in a car park
**SUM UP** Too boring to live with

**USED PARKER'S CHOOSER SAYS...**
**FOR** Equipment; refinement
**AGAINST** Poor economy; sloppy handling; lacks image
**VALUE** Honda's reputation for reliability is a bonus; what kills Legend's appeal is that it lacks prestige

might also be less stressful, depending on how adventurous you are.

Lower pricing, and more aggressive deals by Volkswagen and other manufacturers' UK retail networks, have caused a reduction in the number of enquiries to many importers. Levels of interest also vary according to the age of models.

The Mk 4 VW Golf was for years one of the cars most in demand from importers, but enquiries dipped as it neared the end of its run. The arrival in 2003 of the Mk 5 created renewed interest.

But importers always offer savings of thousands of pounds on mainstream models such as the Peugeot 307, Citroen C5 and Fiat Stilo. Never buy the first one you see. If a car is available from one company with an attractive discount, there could be a better deal elsewhere.

Leading importers list 1,000 or more new and pre-registered cars for 'immediate delivery' and they obtain them from traders in the Republic of Ireland and mainland Europe. Many

people are caught out over the warranty. There is an EU minimum of two years, but in the UK many manufacturers provide cover lasting 36 months. Check when the warranty runs from. The need for specification checks cannot be over emphasised. For example, smartly priced Toyotas from Holland have been offered without CD players.

Security/alarm systems must be 'Thatcham-approved'. This is industry jargon, signifying that a system meets the standards laid down by the Motor Insurance Repair Research Centre at Thatcham, Berks. Because of the level of car crime in Britain, some cars have enhanced security systems and if your import fails to meet the standard, insurance claims could be invalid.

Be clear about what the price includes and insist on that in writing. Delivery or 'miscellaneous' costs are sometimes added by importers. Vigilance, from start to finish, is essential but the result can be a saving far more dramatic than a grand.

 **IMPORTERS**

How adventurous ●●●●●●●●○○

Potential saving ●●●●●●●●○○

**THE GRAND PLAN**
The terrific opportunities to save several grand (and many do) are diminishing because the gap in prices between the UK and the Continent is closing.
*Tactics:* check many websites to compare prices, then talk to the companies to evaluate their ability to fulfil your order.

# INSIDER GUIDE TO IMPORTERS

The companies listed below are members of the British Independent Motor Trade Association (BIMTA) which says members must accept and sign up to a code of conduct. During the association's first three years, only three complaints needed to be passed to BIMTA's legal adviser. BIMTA says the code of conduct is intended to protect members and their customers 'against many of the problems that the less reputable type of dealer tends to create'. Some BIMTA members trade in a wide range of models while others are more specialised. Many BIMTA members have websites which can be traced via an internet search engine such as Google. BIMTA's website (www.bimta.org) contains considerable general guidance about car imports (click on FAQs – frequently asked questions - on the home page). BIMTA head office: 01892 515 425.

| Company Name | Telephone |
| --- | --- |
| **NORTHERN ENGLAND** | |
| BLACKBURN ACI | 01254 278 963 |
| BLACKBURN Eddlestons | 01254 209 687 |
| BOOTLE Motorway Car Auctions | 0151 933 2277 |
| BRADFORD Agora International | 0131627 8944 |
| CLECKHEATON Autobrokers | 01274 875 100 |
| DONCASTER Green Tree Car Centre | 01302 350 341 |
| LEEDS Motormile Finance | 0113 258 0300 |
| LIVERPOOL The UK Importers Club | 0151 486 5005 |
| NEWCASTLE UNDER LYME Autonet Insurance Services | 01782 381 300 |
| NEWCASTLE UNDER LYME Spencer Prestige & Performance | 01782 566 919 |
| PRESTON Gibson's of Brock | 01995 640 542 |
| SKIPTON Midgley Motor Company | 01756 797 652 |
| SLEAFORD Prestige Vehicle Imports | 01529 421 615 |
| WAKEFIELD World Vehicles | 01924 822 835 |
| WIGAN Langtree Garage | 01254 854 240 |
| WINGATE Dick Graham 4x4 | 01429 837 222 |
| **CENTRAL ENGLAND** | |
| BICESTER The Engine | 01869 600 600 |
| BIRMINGHAM Allied Cars | 0121 446 4222 |
| BIRMINGHAM Anglia Forwarding | 0121 789 6622 |

| | |
|---|---|
| BIRMINGHAM Fair Deal Motors | 0121 773 5404 |
| BIRMINGHAM Insurance Factory | 0870 777 8181 |
| CASTLE DONINGTON Charlesworth | 0115 9377 233 |
| CASTLE DONINGTON The Auction Group | 01332 850 309 |
| CHESTER Japcar Imports | 01244 851 133 |
| DERBY Windmill Garage | 01332 831 542 |
| DUDLEY Xtreme Automobiles | 01384 216 108 |
| HARBURY API Engines | 01926 614 522 |
| FALDINGWORTH Limit Corporation | 01672 885 572 |
| KEMPSTON Marston Autos | 01234 855 033 |
| LEICESTER Bob Gerard | 0116 259 2224 |
| NANTWICH Lodge Vehicle Imports | 01270 524 589 |
| NORTHWICH Warrender Sports & Performance Cars | 0845 330 8800 |
| NORWICH PJ Davey | 01508 530 408 |
| NORWICH Pentagon Cars | 01603 662 938 |
| NOTTINGHAM HBS UK | 01623 792 373 |
| STOKE ON TRENT AutoTec | 01782 505 250 |
| STOURBRIDGE Carpoint | 01384 444 477 |
| TIPTON Stuart Spencer Autos | 0121 557 7795 |
| WARRINGTON Choice Motor Company | 01925 811 181 |
| WARWICK U-Save Automotive | 08456 589 777 |
| WEDNESBURY Universal Motor Group | 01789 741 909 |

## SOUTHERN ENGLAND

| | |
|---|---|
| ALTON Park Lane UK | 01420 544 300 |
| ASHFORD Paragon Motor Co | 07736 073903 |
| BASINGSTOKE Duncan Hamilton | 01256 765 000 |
| BATH Importshop UK (Doublecars r us) | 01373 831 470 |
| BRISTOL Car Imports Direct | 0117 966 2212 |
| CANTERBURY Enviroscope | 01303 894 742 |
| EDGWARE Racebeam | 020 8952 2346 |
| EXETER Dream Imports | 07092 110 153 |
| FADLINGWORTH Limit Corporation | 01673 885 572 |
| FARNBOROUGH Magnum Motor Co | 01252 545 941 |
| FOREST ROW Ashdown GB | 01342 822 160 |
| GUILDFORD MJA Car Sales | 1483 566 111 |
| HIGH WYCOMBE Special Car Company | 01494 565 263 |
| HORSHAM Continental Car Company | 01403 217 890 |

| | |
|---|---|
| LANCING Milwards of Lancing | 01903 766 958 |
| LONDON Dandycars.com | 020 8989 8275 |
| LONDON GT Vehicles | 020 8838 6789 |
| LYDD Millfield Garage | 01797 320 555 |
| LYMINGE Futurautos/Japlink | 01303 863 385 |
| MALMESBURY David Hendry Cars | 01666 824 369 |
| MINEHEAD Coastal 4x4 | 01643 706 677 |
| NAILSEA Tett Hamilton | 01275 856 618 |
| NEWBURY Vehicle Buyers Japan | 01635 389 942 |
| NEWTON ABBOTT Torque Imports | 01626 832 590 |
| NORMANDY CCB Sale | 01483 236 770 |
| ONGAR Autoroute | 01245 248 881 |
| PLYMOUTH Performance Cars | 01752 405 050 |
| POOLE Hughes Motor Co | 01202 381 888 |
| RIPLEY Briwel Motors | 01483 223 535 |
| ROMFORD De Stefano | 020 8597 0061 |
| ROMFORD NA Carriage Co | 020 8597 7472 |
| SLOUGH Trade Sales | 01753 773 763 |
| STANMORE Silver Star | 020 8381 2345 |
| SOUTHAMPTON Motorway Car Auctions | 02380 212 178 |
| SOUTHAMPTON Elite International | 02380 511 750 |
| SOUTHAMPTON Hallmarks Garage | 02380 238 252 |
| SOUTHAMPTON SVA UK | 02380 335 120 |
| SOUTHAMPTON Yuwautotrade Logistics | 023 8033 9611 |
| ST ALBANS Coach House Performance Cars | 01727 874 949 |
| WESTON SUPER MARE Import Solutions | 01934 428 149 |

## SCOTLAND

| | |
|---|---|
| DUNBLANE Dicksons of Dunblane | 01786 823 271 |
| EDINBURGH Mackey Trading Co | 0131 558 7670 |
| KIRKCUDBRIGHT St Marys Garage | 01557 330 234 |

## WALES

| | |
|---|---|
| ABERDARE Marpol Vehicles | 01685 876 253 |
| BLACKWOOD Blackwood 4x4 | 01495 231 217 |
| NEWTON Sarn Garage/DAC Sales | 01686 670 718 |

SOURCE: BRITISH INDEPENDENT MOTOR TRADE ASSOCIATION

Chapter 06

# Brokers

The best track down elusive deals but make sure brokers receive only their fee

"Being a broker is all about bringing together a buyer and a seller, and attempting to provide value for both"

Anything, it is said, is available if you are prepared to pay the price and brokers will tell you the same. The price, of course, is intended to be much lower than if you bought a car in a more conventional way.

There are two kinds of brokers. One is an individual or company with good connections and proven business practice. The other is a shady version of this, out to get your money and hoodwink the authorities along the way. By using common sense (some things are too good to be true), it is possible to distinguish between the two. It is also important to remember that dealing with someone in Holland can be

far safer than finding a broker in the UK. Establish the existence of good business credentials before parting with a penny.

Brokers are close to importers in the way they work. The main difference is they probably hold little or no stock. If you are particular about an exact derivative, colour and specification of, say, an Audi TT, they will provide one for you. Other companies may have stock, or a regular supply, and this means you will wait for less time.

The rule that must never be broken is to always pay the dealer (possibly based in mainland Europe) directly for the car and ensure the broker only gets their fee. Good brokers state this unequivocally in their ads and on their websites. They ask for a deposit of around 10 per cent to dissuade people from placing orders with a number of firms, buying from the first able to supply, and leaving the rest with unwanted cars. Private buyers can behave as badly as dealers.

Some brokers buy cars from contract hire and lease fleets and sell them to car supermarkets and dealers. They will sell to private buyers after adding a mark-up for their trouble. Brokers also buy direct from manufacturers left with a bottleneck of cars due to disappointing sales and then distribute them to supermarkets. Being a broker is all about bringing together a seller and buyer, and attempting to provide value for both.

To be successful in dealing with brokers, it helps to be aware of economic and other changes throughout the EU. If your broker was buying from a supplier in Germany in 2002/03, it was useful to realise the country was in recession and that businesses were going bust. You know that supply will often exceed demand, and this should be reflected in lower prices.

Smart car brokers can spot new models that initially will not be able to satisfy demand. They then supply individuals within an agreed time and at the agreed price. Brokers thus offer a range of services, and you pay accordingly.

Some will provide the basic service of identifying a foreign dealer who can supply the car and arrange the deposit, leaving you to do the rest. Maybe that is all the help you need, but these dealers on the Continent can be traced relatively easily enough through magazines. A number of them (based in the UK and abroad) are listed here and a good source for others is *Carbuyer*, a magazine that began life as *Car Import Guide* and is closest to the people and companies arranging parallel and grey imports. Foreign brokers/importers advertising in the UK normally have staff who speak

## TOM HARTLEY'S FIVE TOP BROKER TIPS

Tom Hartley has been in business in Derbyshire for 30 years buying and selling sporting and luxury cars such as Rolls-Royces, Ferraris and Porsches, mainly for clients with precise requirements (colour, specification etc). He believes buyers of more modestly priced cars are entitled to expect brokers to deal with them in the way he treats his customers. This is his insider guide to finding a good broker:

1 Be sure they are a solid business operator, not someone selling fruit and veg off a stall last month who now sees a chance to make money with a few deals.
2 Ask them to prove how long they have been in business as a car broker.
3 Demand a bank reference. Walk away if one is not provided.
4 Never do business with someone who asks for cash. It probably means there is something wrong.
5 Rely on your judgement when assessing whether the broker can be trusted. I only see people by appointment, however wealthy they are. You must respect and trust a broker.

www.tomhartley.com
01283 762 762

English. For many, that facility will be regarded as essential.

For a full door-to-door service, you need an agent who will locate the car, bring it to Britain, negotiate it through Customs & Excise and deliver it to your home or workplace. They will handle UK registration, payment of VAT and arrange car tax, too. A few dealers in mainland Europe also offer a similar service as exporters.

Brokers spend much of their time on mobile phones searching for cars. They scour auction stock and bid for a known buyer or, from time to time, on a hunch. When you make an enquiry, they will point to the advantage of buying one of the cars they have in stock to minimise delay. This has the advantage for them of keeping stock moving and aiding cash flow.

A disadvantage in the eyes of some potential customers is that you cannot trade in your existing car with a broker. You are left with the hassle of selling privately and co-ordinating the transactions so you can stay mobile without the cost of hiring a car. Selling privately is likely to attract a higher price than in a part exchange and this can be added to the fund when buying. A few weeks begging lifts or using public transport may be worthwhile.

A trading method like brokering inevitably attracts rogues who will take advantage of the unwary. In one scam, dodgy brokers fail to register for VAT, charge the 17.5 per cent (£3,500 on every £20,000 paid for a car) and move on after six months to trade under another name before Customs & Excise catches up with them. Avoid anyone using only a mobile phone number and ask for a business address. Visit them if possible. Also, form a judgement of the person you talk to. If they are evasive, they probably have something to hide.

Ask for a business reference such as a bank, because an honest trader will be happy to provide the details. You may have to pay a fee to the bank but it will provide peace of mind. Another ploy to be avoided is paying a large deposit, possibly up to 30 per cent, which is held while delivery might be

## GRAND CONTENDER

## LAND ROVER FREELANDER

### ▤ NEW CAR SAYS...
**FOR** Painless on-road
**AGAINST** Pointless off-road
**SUM UP** Elastic brand engineering

### 👍 USED (1993-2001)
### PARKER'S CHOOSER SAYS...
**FOR** The badge; frugal Td4 diesel; off-road ability
**AGAINST** Thirsty V6; quite expensive to buy
**VALUE** Balance of road manners and off-road ability; Station Wagon the family choice; Softback more macho

## GRAND CONTENDER

### JEEP CHEROKEE

**NEW CAR SAYS...**
**FOR** Tough, rugged, king of the school run
**AGAINST** Thirsty, old-fashioned
**SUM UP** Get soft-roader instead

**USED (1993-2001)**
**PARKER'S CHOOSER SAYS...**
**FOR** Tough and well equipped
**AGAINST** Running costs
**VALUE** A versatile alternative to a family estate; used prices are falling faster now

the word 'trader' or a capital T to conform to advertising standards. The ones to avoid pose as private sellers. It is best to ask the direct question when responding to the ad.

Some buyers get themselves into trouble because they are too greedy. If the quoted savings are substantially more than those offered elsewhere, then there are probably grounds for suspicion. The emotional element of car purchase is amplified when tracking down an exclusive model for a price that will impress friends or business associates. The best chance of success comes when you strip out emotion, use logic and exercise patience.

Other aspects of buying through a broker also require care. Ask who is responsible for the currency risk in case the exchange rate changes appreciably between when you agree a price and the day the car is delivered. Take care not to be caught between the broker and the supplying dealer, with you losing out.

If the car is coming from a foreign dealer, insist on talking to them before placing an order. If the broker refuses to allow this, walk away from the deal.

Deposits should be by credit card because any payment between £100 and £30,000 paid to a trader in this way is covered by the Consumer Credit Act 1974. This protects you from losing your money if the supplier goes out of business. Ask your credit card company for more details. Use an escrow (third party) account for the final balance (your bank will help with this).

Bear in mind that a handsome saving today on a car will pull down its future value. This is one of the many

delayed for as long as six months. The money should be gaining interest in your savings account, not that of the agent or dealer. Brokers who advertise in motoring magazines and motoring sections of newspapers, including the *Daily Telegraph* and the *Sunday Times*, are more likely to be trustworthy. Advertising staff run checks if they are suspicious and their experience helps them to identify traders likely to bring the publication into disrepute.

Small ads placed by legitimate brokers and others operating a business to sell Jaguar convertibles and other prestige cars should include

# INSIDER BROKER DATABASE*

Alliance Car Imports
www.alliancecarimports.co.uk
01254 399 310

BMW Imports
www.bmwimports.net
020 8473 4150

British Car Imports
www.britishcarimports.com
0049 4815 998 279

Car Import Solutions
www.carimportsolutions.co.uk
01274 580 097

Carproviders
www.carproviders.co.uk
01234 218 120

Epic Vehicle Sourcing
www.wesaveyoumoney.co.uk
0800 980 90 90

EuropSave
www.europsave.co.uk
01256 398 822

Eurekar
www.eurekar.com
0870 126 5336

Euro Imports
www.euroimportsuk.com
01243 554 477

Exclusive Euro Car Imports
www.exclusive-eurocar.co.uk
08700 550 800

Fastracker Cars
www.fastracker.uk.com
01473 749 911

Garage De Zutter (Belgium)
www.fordknokke.com
0032 5061 4444

Hallmark International
www.hallmark-international.co.uk
0191 218 0020

Import Car Search
www.importcarsearch.com
020 8992 7361

Netherlands Car Trading
www.nct.nl
0031 30 247 5111

Teal Car Imports
www.tealcarimports.com
0191 416 8589

The Personal Import Co.
www.personalimport.co.uk
01244 344 544

* Inclusion in this list does not suggest a recommendation and other companies may be as good or better.

unpalatable economic rules of car ownership because you should expect the buyer (especially a dealer during a trade-in) to ask why the car was first registered in Holland. They will know it cost you less than the UK recommended retail price and adjust the transaction price accordingly.

So you might, said one broker, pocket a £2,500 saving but lose £1,500 of that when you come to trade-in or sell after two or three years. It is another reason for trying to squeeze a lower price out of your neighbourhood dealer.

## BROKERS

How adventurous ● ● ● ● ● ● ● ● ● ●
Potential saving ● ● ● ● ● ● ● ● ○ ○

### THE GRAND PLAN
Substantial savings are possible if you can find a good honest broker. The best of the breed will find the car you want and deliver it to you. Real brokers carry little or no stock.
*Tactics:* be suspicious, insist on references, always pay the price of the car directly to the supplier. The broker only gets their fee.

Chapter 07

# Ex rental/fleet cars

### Hard-worked cars that have much to appeal to private buyers, as operators are beginning to realise

"Some people take items for their own use – rental firms have to check that hubcaps and floor mats are in place"

People are understandably cautious when considering the purchase of an ex-fleet car, but popular misconceptions abound. Just as diesels are still regarded by an ill-informed minority as congenitally inferior to petrol-powered equivalents, so ex-fleet cars are often viewed as clapped-out and a high-risk purchase.

This is far from the case. Fleet cars, though normally covering far more miles over their first three years than those privately owned, often spend much of their time enjoying stress-free motorway cruising, and are regularly serviced and maintained. An increasing proportion of diesel cars, noted for their length of devoted service, together with the continuing all-round rise in reliability, add to the appeal of three-year-old cars for private motorists. So much so that rental fleet operators and contract hire and lease companies are seeking to capitalise on the value in cars after three years.

In itself this suggests private motorists should give serious consideration to ex-fleet cars. But before buying, be sure to check the equipment. Some people who rent cars steal items, proving that the trade does not have all the rogues (manufacturers remove anything detachable to prevent thefts from motor show display cars, too).

Rental firms supplying cars to private and business drivers for a day, week or fortnight buy some of them and, in effect, 'rent' others from manufacturers. Many cars are supplied under short-term agreements that end with the manufacturer buying them back at an agreed price. The rental market is closely tied up with short-term measures taken by manufacturers to improve the look of their sales performance. This is a fast-moving and frantic sector of the market.

The role of re-marketing companies, specialising in locating trade buyers for ex-fleet cars, is sometimes made more difficult by manufacturers' activities. A limited edition model, announced without warning, immediately deflates the value of the list derivative that is coming off rental fleets without bonus features such as alloy wheels and air conditioning.

Model changes also dramatically affect values. A Vauxhall Vectra with a list price of around £15,000 was worth about £7,500 in 2002 after six or nine months on a rental fleet. In 2003, the value over the same period was £10,500 because it was the all-new Vectra.

According to Glass's Information Services (a trade adviser on vehicle values), metallic paint makes little difference to the value because it is virtually standard on rental cars. But on a Ford Focus Zetec, air conditioning adds anything from £300 to £700 (more than it was worth new). One bonus in buying an ex-rental car is that it may well have an acoustic parking aid, fitted to reduce the risk of parking knocks by renters unused to the size of the model.

Glass's advises rental companies to remove anything that is not firmly attached to cars, including parcel shelves and luggage nets. Because some renters think it is fair game to take items for their own use, rental firms are advised to check that hubcaps and floor mats are in place when the car is returned. And, would you believe, to count the removable seats in MPVs.

A typical fleet car, such as a Renault Laguna or Vauxhall Astra, will on average sell for as much as £700 more on a retail site than it would at auction. Cars that have been on rental fleets only briefly have a special retail appeal denied to the huge number run on company fleets often for three years.

## GRAND CONTENDER

### PEUGEOT 307

**NEW** CAR SAYS...
**FOR** European Car of the year
**AGAINST** Last year (2002)
**SUM UP** Decent quality and stylish too

**USED** PARKER'S CHOOSER SAYS...
**FOR** Build quality; excellent ride; safety equipment
**AGAINST** Steering lacks feel; petrol models lack refinement
**VALUE** Feels well built; all except basic cars well equipped

Even so, ex-fleet cars with anything from 60,000 to 100,000 miles behind them are refurbished to a high standard prior to auction. They can be bargain buys for private motorists willing to risk their judgement when buying one that goes 'under the hammer' (see chapter 9).

Ex-rental cars have traditionally been sold through franchised dealers, at car supermarkets, via auctions or online but rental firms are starting to sell direct, both to private buyers and the trade.

Hertz, the world's largest vehicle

rental company, operating from more than 7,000 locations in over 150 countries, has been testing the UK retail market in a modest way since the late 1990s. It has centres at Carrington (Manchester, opened 1998) Didcot (Oxfordshire,1999), and Linwood (Glasgow, 2000) because retail sales yield more than disposal via auction. Hertz will not reveal the size of its fleet, nor the number of cars available for retail sale each year. But it is expected to expand its retail operation.

The combined operation holds a stock of hundreds of cars for retail sale but the centres are primarily geared to selling to trade. The hush-hush Hertz retail business, mentioned only on its website, restricts choice mainly to various Ford and Mazda models. This is hardly surprising because Hertz is part of Ford Motor Company, which has a controlling management interest in Mazda of Japan.

In marketing its direct sales, Hertz plays on the appeal of nearly-new cars by emphasising the early depreciation when cars are bought new. 'With a nearly-new Hertz vehicle, you beat that high depreciation because we've already absorbed it,' runs the patter. It is, however, no more than a bit of marketing blarney because Hertz acquires Ford and Mazda cars at heavily discounted prices. The world's largest private fleet purchaser of vehicles worldwide also has enormous clout in doing deals with other manufacturers.

Hertz normally keeps cars in the UK for six months or 15,000 miles, whichever comes first. A six-month-old

## GRAND CONTENDER

### MERCEDES-BENZ E-CLASS

**NEW** CAR SAYS...
**FOR** nice to drive, well equipped
**AGAINST** Pricey, plasticky cabin
**SUM UP** Best 5-series alternative

**USED** (1995-2002)
PARKER'S CHOOSER SAYS...
**FOR** Prestige; longevity; integrity; low depreciation
**AGAINST** Pricey; plasticky cabin
**VALUE** You'll never regret buying quality; good long-term prospect

## GRAND CONTENDER

## LEXUS LS

### 📖 NEW CAR SAYS...

**FOR** Probably the best
equipped car in the world
**AGAINST** Breeze block styling
**SUM UP** Viable S-class
alternative

### 📖 USED (1990-2000)
### PARKER'S CHOOSER SAYS...

**FOR** All-round abilities; beats
rivals on price
**AGAINST** Keen drivers may be
disappointed
**VALUE** Better value than
GS300; worthy rival to 7-Series,
A8 or S-Class if you're not after
ultimate driving experience

Alamo and other rivals, Hertz has to look after its cars because business and leisure customers regard breakdowns with equal contempt. Avis disposes of its ex-fleet cars through Yourautochoice, part of the Autobytel website.

For manufacturers, rental operations are a valuable means of enticing potential customers to try new models. The buy-back agreements enable rental operators to work out their expenditure over the period with considerable accuracy, as long as they can attract sufficient customers. When manufacturers take the cars back, they will be refurbished and then supplied to their dealers who sell them through a branded scheme, such as Ford Direct. The system works ideally if a model has both quality and customer appeal as this produces a series of profit margins for manufacturer, rental company and dealer.

Rental agreements are widely used by manufacturers to dispose of cars that are not selling well through their dealer networks. The greater the difficulty in selling the model, the bigger the discount extracted from the manufacturer.

The Easy Group, which through EasyJet forced down the price of air travel, decided in the late 1990s to get into car rental and wanted to make an impact that would attract publicity.

In 2000, Easy signed a headline-grabbing agreement to equip its fleet with 5,000 Mercedes cars. All the cars were the Mercedes A-class, widely praised for its innovative design but perceived as expensive for its size, despite the Mercedes badge. Figures were never revealed, but Easy

car with three years warranty remaining will be sold with enough cover to look after the needs of many private buyers before they want to replace it.

Before sale, Hertz gives the cars a 12,000-mile service and full valet. Many potential customers will have experienced Hertz when renting a car on holiday, adding to the positive marketing image.

Like Avis, National Car Rental,

extracted a sizeable discount from Mercedes. And it gave the prestige manufacturer a guaranteed outlet for thousands of A-class cars that were not selling as well as planned in the UK and elsewhere in Europe. For Mercedes, there was the bonus of raising awareness in the car through rental bookings.

At the end of their Easy life, the A-class cars return to Mercedes which offers them to its dealers as used stock. Prices can be adjusted more easily and with greater flexibility than with new cars. But this all comes at a price to Mercedes, whose iconic badge probably carries more weight than any other. The A-Class was launched as the clever car for families who believed they could never afford a 'Merc', but the rental deal has devalued the model.

Contract hire and leasing companies have mixed views about selling ex-fleet cars directly to private buyers. The hassle factor has to be weighed against potential profit and policy can change. Lex Vehicles, now known as RAC plc following the acquisition of the motoring services company, initially acquired and operated a number of retail sites to

## GRAND CONTENDER

### PORSCHE BOXSTER

### NEW CAR SAYS...
**FOR** Stunning to drive, great to own, gorgeous
**AGAINST** Nothing serious
**SUM UP** Work of genius

### USED
**PARKER'S CHOOSER SAYS...**
**FOR** Affordable – for a Porsche; handling; style
**AGAINST** High used prices
**VALUE** Relatively cheap for a Porsche but with all qualities intact

 ## INSIDER EX-RENTAL DATABASE

**Hertz Car Sales**
www.hertz.co.uk
(click on car sales)
01235 824 000

**Avis**
www.yourautohoice.com
(clicking on new, nearly new or used cars, provides a link to the Autobytel website)
0800 783 1514

**INSIDER GUIDE TO FLEET SALES**

The variation between fleet sales in 2002 and 2001 provides an indication of makes and models favoured by drivers of company cars. They look for driver appeal and refinement, combined with the reliability also sought by companies anxious to keep their staff mobile. Supplies to fleet operators, even if heavily discounted, count in the same way as retail sales when manufacturers claim 'record success'.

## TOP TEN FLEET MARKET MANUFACTURER 2002

| Company Name | 2002 sales | 2001 sales | variation |
|---|---|---|---|
| 1 Ford | 221,255 | 223,231 | - 0.89% |
| 2 Vauxhall | 214,206 | 201,460 | + 6.33% |
| 3 Renault | 102,272 | 87,582 | +16.77% |
| 4 Peugeot | 92,228 | 86,692 | + 6.39% |
| 5 Volkswagen | 81,096 | 70,131 | +15.64% |
| 6 Nissan | 52,571 | 53,732 | -2.15% |
| 7 Citroen | 38,580 | 42,385 | - 8.98% |
| 8 Toyota | 37,740 | 29,506 | + 27.91% |
| 9 BMW | 35,502 | 34,304 | +3.49% |
| 10 Fiat | 33,448 | 41,097 | -18.51% |

SOURCE: FLEET NEWS

## TOP 10 FLEET MODELS 2002

| Company Name | 2002 sales | 2001 sales versus 2001 |
|---|---|---|
| 1 Ford Focus | 101,399 | +7.17% |
| 2 Vauxhall Astra | 75,190 | +6.92% |
| 3 Ford Mondeo | 58,314 | -7.84% |
| 4 Vauxhall Corsa | 53,303 | +23.27% |
| 5 Vauxhall Vectra | 47,989 | -14.71% |
| 6 Renault Megane | 40,654 | -6.37% |
| 7 Renault Clio | 33,446 | +25.08% |
| 8 Volkswagen Golf | 32,642 | +17.21% |
| 9 Ford Fiesta | 30,970 | -11.7% |
| 10 Peugeot 206 | 30,000 | +21.74% |

SOURCE: FLEET NEWS

dispose of cars coming off its large fleet of vehicles leased to businesses, but then sold them.

In 2002 and 2003, two high street banks caused a stir in the retail motor industry by acquiring major car dealer groups. You might find yourself borrowing money from a high street bank that controls the contract hire/leasing group that previously owned the car you are buying.

The Royal Bank of Scotland (RBS) paid £110m for Dixon Motors, the seventh largest UK motor retail group with a turnover of more than £800m, in 2002. Dixon supplies cars to insurer Direct Line that runs internet-based Jamjar car sales (see chapter 4). An even more interesting link is to Lombard Vehicle Management, a company that each year disposes of 20,000 cars from its fleet. Many of these are sold through Dixon dealerships.

Next came the £48.7m purchase of Dutton Forshaw, a top 20 dealer group with annual sales of around £500m, by Lloyds TSB, owners of Autolease. Many Autolease ex-fleet cars will be sold through Dutton Forshaw's 40 or so dealerships, so be sure to ask what the car you are interested in has been doing for the previous three years.

Add Lloyds TSB's ownership of Black Horse Motor Finance to the equation and you have a heaven-made virtuous business circle that should generate more profit than a number of equivalent but unconnected businesses.

Car buyers should always attempt to turn these links to their own advantage. If you have accounts with the Royal Bank of Scotland, it is worth asking how taking on a loan is going to help you to do a better deal when buying from one of their Dutton Forshaw dealerships.

Car purchase generates so much revenue that the influence of banks was always likely to become a factor. The importance of cars to their

 ## INSIDER GUIDE: WHEN TO BUY A USED CAR

This table is advice to companies about when to dispose of fleet cars. Private buyers should demand lower than average prices if cars have higher mileages than these.

### PETROL

2 years: up to 40,000 miles
3 years: up to 60,000 miles
4 years: up to 70,000 miles

### DIESEL

2 years: up to 60,000 miles
3 years: up to 80,000 miles
4 years: up to 80,000 miles

SOURCE: MANHEIM AUCTIONS

customers, and the high level of money spent, is expected to lead to banks becoming more directly involved in motor retailing. This is logical because manufacturers make good money from providing motor finance to private buyers.

·····➤ **EX-RENTAL/FLEET SALES**

How adventurous  ● ● ● ● ● ● ○ ○ ○ ○

Potential saving  ● ● ● ● ● ● ● ○ ○ ○

**THE GRAND PLAN**
This method requires effort because most ex-rental fleet cars return to manufacturers in short-term buy-back deals, although operators are exploring retail sales.
Tactics: check Hertz prices and compare them with car supermarkets.

## Chapter 08

# Used car dealers

The stock they hold invites hard bargaining by
private buyers – marked prices are a starting point

"You have right and the law on your side when giving
shady dealers a difficult time"

Between 6m and 7m
used cars are sold in
Britain each year. In
your quest for the
right one, you barely
scratch the
surface of a
massive market,
that has
hundreds of
thousands of
similar cars in
need of an owner.

A car becomes 'used' the second it is driven away from a showroom. At that moment, it has lost some value. Try to sell it the next day and people expect a discount. Even at that early stage, the suspicions surrounding a used car would be evident. There has to be something wrong with it, we always believe.

The pick of used cars are sold either through dealers holding the franchise to sell the make new, via specialist traders in posh brands, or privately. Lucky is the driver who gets an aunt's four-year-old supermini with 8,000 miles on the clock. Millions of

other cars are auctioned, go to car supermarkets or are sold privately.

Volume manufacturers run branded used car schemes in partnership with their dealers, with links from the car makers' websites. Vauxhall led the way with the launch in 1991 of Network Q that sells all makes and offers a handy way for dealers to maximise the value of trade-ins. In year one, Network Q sales totalled 40,600. In 2002 it had trebled to a record 122,709. There was a marked increase in Network Q enquiries via the Vauxhall website providing more evidence that car buyers feel comfortable using an internet sales medium associated with a familiar brand.

Many trade-in cars go to big supermarkets, or to traders offering only a dozen or so used vehicles. For some people, supermarkets are no-go areas because of their intimidating size, while too many used car outlets look depressing with their fluttering plastic flags and graffiti-strewn walls.

Because these businesses end up with stock that has no special value, you have the opportunity to negotiate hard. The staff may well be aware that more cars are arriving the next day and are under pressure to keep stock moving. This is 'move the metal' land and retail buyers hold all the cards.

But you need to tread carefully. The used car business still has much to do to clean up its act. In 2003, secondhand car dealers were given their toughest warning yet by the Office of Fair Trading. In effect, it told them: 'Deal unfairly with consumers and your licence to trade will be removed.'

You have right and the law on your side when giving shady traders a difficult time. By asking to see their consumer credit licence (issued under the Consumer Credit Act 1974), you make them aware of your knowledge and reduce the odds against being sold a suspect car.

You are most likely to run into trouble when buying from traders with a dozen cars priced from £499. Many firms like these have been forced out of business following prosecutions by local trading standard department officials or by competition from reputable retailers. There are exceptions and some are fledgling businesses run by

## INSIDER GUIDE TO BUYERS' RIGHTS ON DEALER SALES

- Legal rights enforceable only against a business in existence, so look for an established recommended business for security
- Car must conform to any description it has been given or representation made regarding its condition or history (such as 'reconditioned engine')
- Car must be of 'satisfactory quality and fit for the purpose intended' and meet the standard expected for its description, price, age and mileage
- This requirement cannot be excluded with signs such as 'sold as seen'. Failure to comply is a breach of your rights, for which you may be entitled to compensation or your money back
- Terms of warranty/mechanical breakdown insurance agreements vary but usually exclude 'wear and tear'. They may also have a limit on the amount of each claim. It is essential to check terms you are entitled to
- The rights detailed above are independent of each other. If you are not covered under one heading, try another

SOURCE: RAC

## INSIDER GUIDE TO TRADING STANDARDS

The Office of Fair Trading says the motor trade accounted for nearly a third of all action taken over infringements to trading licences in 2002. The OFT published 'guidance' for car dealers that calls into question a trader's fitness to hold a licence. The guidance is aimed primarily at secondhand car dealers but, where appropriate, also applies to franchised dealers in new cars. If you have suspicions about a dealer, a reference to these OFT concerns can persuade him to be more open.

young entrepreneurs who will go on to achieve success.

Get a feel for used car traders in your area by studying the ads in your local paper. Look for companies that have been around for 20 or 30 years as they might have acquired a decent reputation, or for those advertising 30 to 50 cars, which suggests they have the financial resources to hold a reasonable stock. The mere fact they are advertising each week for a month indicates they are paying their bills to the newspaper publisher.

Be careful when a sole low-mileage, three-year-old Mercedes is highlighted among a crop of M, N, P and S plated

cheap cars as it is probably being sold by one of the staff or an associate to lift the image of the outlet.

The wording of the ads can provide useful clues before you bother visiting the site. 'We've EXTENDED these offers whilst stocks last!!!' is a gem because it is a barely disguised way of saying: 'We're DESPERATE to sell these cars and will knock lots off the advertised price'.

'Vouchers' proclaiming '£200 discount off every used car – must be presented at time of negotiation' are often incorporated into ads and are meaningless. The salesman will merely make an adjustment downwards on the part exchange deal offered, or the minimum amount he will take for the car.

Another approach is an advertised '£2,000 minimum trade-in – any age, no MoT, no problem' against a choice of cars of similar type, age and condition. Again, the final transaction price will be the same as it would have been without this sales ploy.

Or an ad might state a 'balance to change from only £3,999' against 'a price when new of £11,500'. This is cleverer because it plays on our wish to find something for nothing or, at least, a great bargain. The ad contrasts the apparent low price (though note the 'from only') with a much higher sale price.

The cars for sale are likely to be three-year-old ex-fleet stock that have little appeal. You are supposed to focus on the low balance to pay rather than finding a car you really want and will enjoy driving. The car should drive the deal, not the so-called bargain price.

All marked prices are a starting

point for negotiation wherever you buy, but especially at non-franchised used car dealerships. They will often be prepared to sell poor stock at or below what they paid when they want to make room for better cars coming in which offer the prospect of a quicker sale and a larger profit. Salesmen will not admit it, but if you adopt that assumption it will help you to drive down the price.

Some larger used car groups separate more modern stock from cheaper cars by selling them from two outlets. Low-price cars might be sold

for £100 to £3,500 from a 'quality part exchanges centre'. At this price level, people are tempted to dispense with an engineer's report (normally costing £100 or more) because it is out of proportion to the amount being paid for the car.

In all price bands, salesmen may try to put customers off getting an independent assessment claiming the sale cannot be delayed because other people are interested in the car. This always creates a dilemma for a buyer. But losing the chance to buy a good car is better than hastily acquiring a bad one. The AA and RAC realise the urgency and try to conduct surveys within two days of the request.

Walking away from the chance of buying a half-price car can be a good idea because deals that look too good to be true are invariably exactly that. Though complex, the car sales business is controlled by one simple economic law: the bigger the discount when you buy, the greater the likely rate of fall in the value of the car over the following two or three years. New cars that are heavily discounted because of modest genuine demand suffer greater depreciation than those sold at full price to eager buyers. In the period 2000-2003, used car values suffered because of the continuing rise in new car sales as manufacturers ramped up offers to customers while interest rates were low and economic indicators buoyant.

A league table produced by Glass's Information Services, a company assessing current and future car values for the trade, analyses trends in values between 2000-2003 (see panel). This shows how top coupes like

## KEY ISSUES COVERED BY THE OFT

- Vehicle roadworthiness including altering the construction of a vehicle (such as 'cut and shut' – parts of two cars welded together) and providing stolen or fraudulent MoT documents
- False or misleading descriptions including verbal claims, altering mileages and misrepresenting the specification or history of a vehicle
- Vehicle ownership, such as supplying a vehicle with an outstanding finance agreement or a cloned vehicle (stolen car with number plates taken from a legitimate vehicle)
- Traders claiming to be private sellers

\* SOURCE: OFT

the Audi TT lose a third of their value over three years, while large cars like the Peugeot 607 are shedding two-thirds. Cars in the Vauxhall Astra and Ford Mondeo sectors of the market barely do better, according to Glass's.

The value of this survey is that it contrasts the proportion of value one car holds against another. For example, sports utility vehicles like the Toyota RAV4 do better than big luxury cars such as the Mercedes S-class. The trend is toward smaller cars (see chapter 15 - an ever-changing industry).

The Glass's research for the trade provides insider knowledge about different types of cars and market trends that will influence prices you can expect to pay on the used market. It shows that:

• High values of used niche cars, such as coupes, convertibles and sports utility vehicles will be eroded as more models are introduced

 ## RESIDUAL VALUE (RV) LEAGUE TABLE

% = percentage of the price when new that, on average, is retained after three years

| Model/example | 2003 | | 2000 | |
| --- | --- | --- | --- | --- |
| | RV% | rank | RV% | rank |
| Top coupes Audi TT | 63.8% | 1 | 57.2% | 2 |
| Top convertibles BMW 3 series | 62.0% | 2 | 66.7% | 1 |
| Convertibles MGF | 51.2% | 3 | 54.2% | 3 |
| SUV Toyota RAV4 | 49.1% | 4 | 44.1% | 9 |
| Compact MPV Citroen Picasso | 48.5% | 5 | not applicable | |
| 4x4 Land Rover Discovery 4 | 7.4% | 6 | 44.7% | 8 |
| Premium upper medium Audi A4 | 47.1% | 7 | 45.8% | 6 |
| Full MPVs SEAT Alhambra | 45.8% | 8= | 45.5% | 7 |
| Premium large BMW 5 Series | 45.8% | 8= | 53.0% | 4 |
| Supermini Nissan Micra | 41.5% | 10 | 42.1% | 11 |
| Coupes Ford Puma | 40.7% | 11 | 51.3% | 5 |
| Luxury Mercedes S-Class | 38.8% | 12 | 43.4% | 10 |
| Lower medium Vauxhall Astra | 37.6% | 13 | 39.1% | 12 |
| Upper medium Ford Mondeo | 34.6% | 14 | 33.7% | 14 |
| Large car Peugeot 607 | 31.3% | 15 | 34.1% | 13 |

SOURCE: GLASS'S INFORMATION SERVICES

- Lower transaction prices (what you pay, not the car's list price) and special offers by manufacturers (free loans etc) will keep pushing down residuals (value retained by cars)
- It will be difficult for supermini residuals to improve because so many cars are sold in this sector. And entry prices (cheapest in the range) keep falling as manufacturers chase sales
- There was a rise of 1 per cent in values of upper medium cars (industry jargon for models like the Ford Mondeo and Vauxhall Vectra) because more were sold in 2000 than in 2002
- Even values of convertibles suffered because leading models like the MGF and Mazda MX5 were ageing.
- Coupe values 'behaved disastrously', says Glass's, which blames ageing products and a weakening demand for coupe-styled cars (apart from 'top coupes' – see below)
- Residuals of 4x4s like the Land Rover Discovery improved by 3 per cent. Glass's says: 'This can largely be attributed to families wanting a

second vehicle to transport their offspring; often mileage covered is low so fuel consumption becomes a lesser issue. This goes hand in hand with perceived safety'
- The desirability of top coupes (such as the Audi TT) has been growing and their residuals climbed 6.6 per cent
- There are few buyers for used luxury and premium large cars because of the high running costs
- Full-size multi-purpose vehicles (MPVs such as the SEAT Alhambra) have held values well despite increasing numbers. They are popular with rental and taxi firms and among families who use them for holidays
- Values of sports utility vehicles (SUVs) were strong between 2000 and 2003 with the Land Rover Freelander, Toyota RAV4 and Honda CRV dominating the sector
- Residuals of compact MPVs (such as Citroen Picasso) are likely to start falling back as, from 2003, large numbers leave fleets to be sold in the retail market

 **USED CAR DEALERS**

How adventurous  ●●●●●●●○○○
Potential saving  ●●●●●●●○○○

**THE GRAND PLAN**
For 'adventurous' read "hard work". A genuine saving involves seeking out the car you want at a lower cost than something comparable.
Tactics: extensive research into what is on offer and the use of a price guide.

## Chapter 09

# Auctions

### The potential for success is considerable if you stick to the rules that work and accept the risks

"Auction companies welcome retail buyers because they invariably pay more for a car than the trade"

Buying a car at auction is at the top end of the stress scale for most private motorists, and the incentive for heading there is entirely financial for most people. But the experience is exciting for some and a few would not buy in any other way because of the big savings on offer.

Auction rooms are traditionally the haunt of trade buyers and some resent outsiders trying to cherry-pick the choicest cars. The professionals buy today, tomorrow, or whenever the cars

and prices are right. A private buyer wants to make an instant killing on a single car. There are signs of increasing interest among private buyers as the market opens up and people weigh risk and an enjoyable retail experience against savings.

The auction business is geared to serve fleet operators and the motor trade, whereas you are searching for a single car. The wholesale buyers are there to stock their own businesses, or to enrich the mix of a group, but rarely have specific buyers in mind. They work in much the same way as traders bidding for a crop of pineapples. They know some of the fruit will be rotten but, on balance, there is a profit to be made.

Private buyers at auction go to acquire a car for themselves, or maybe a son, aunt or friend. They have a key advantage: they do not have to stop bidding at a price that allows for reselling at a profit. They may, though, be buying the rotten fruit.

So the potential for success is considerable as long as you stick to the rules that work, accept the risks, and are prepared to back your judgement without the comfort of a safety net. This channel to market requires nerve and some people love the idea of a big saving by snatching a choice car from the grasp of the motor trade.

Britain's car auction market is dominated by two big groups with a total of 42 car auction centres in the UK. BCA Europe and Manheim Europe have a reputation in the trade for fierce competition, both in auction halls and online. BCA Europe's 23 auction centres handle a million vehicles a year in the UK, although some are moved on to other outlets. Manheim offers 500,000 vehicles annually in 19 UK centres and three in France. There are also dozens of smaller car auction operators and risks are reduced by dealing with members of the Society of Motor Auctions (see panel).

Auction companies welcome retail buyers because they invariably pay more for a car than the trade. These companies are staffed to handle the trade buyers, not the small minority of retail customers, but there should at least be a 'how to bid and buy' pack available, and staff will normally attempt to be helpful.

Private motorists need to know they are up against wholesalers armed with key commercial information, trade data and probably plenty of experience and who are prepared to bide their time for the right deal. The professionals fixing a bidding limit on a high-mileage ex-fleet car might know that, in another 5,000 miles, it will be due for a part replacement costing around £500. They also buy monthly valuation updates and this puts them in a strong position because they fix a realistic commercial ceiling price in their mind. Nothing is likely to persuade them to exceed it.

## AUCTION COMPANY SELLING DESCRIPTIONS
### (AND WHAT THEY MEAN)

**No major mechanical faults**
This should include engine, gearbox, clutch, brakes, steering and transmission. Complaints must be made to the auction engineer within an hour of the auction ending.

**Specified faults**
The auctioneer reads out faults notified by the seller. Complaints about major mechanical faults, other than those specified, must be made within an hour of the auction ending.

**Sold as seen and with all its faults**
These are bought as they are with no warranties from the seller. No complaints entertained under any circumstances.

**On an engineer's report**
This is compiled by the auction company at the request of the seller, and is on display prior to sale. Post-sale complaints must relate to wrong descriptions in the report.

SOURCE: BCA EUROPE

## INSIDER GUIDE TO AUCTION BUYING

A private motorist who has bought five cars at auction for himself and members of his family reveals the tactics that work.

- You need to get a buzz from the experience if it is going to work for you. At the very least treat a visit to a car auction as an enjoyable day out.
- Chat to the member of staff who drives the car you fancy into the auction area, listen for splutters as the engine is started and watch out for puffs of blue smoke from the exhaust.
- Do not be put off by cars that have minor adaptations for a disabled driver because equipment can often be removed cheaply and easily.
- Beware of cars, especially diesels, that have been used as taxis. Especially look out for holes in the dashboard left after the removal of two-way radios.
- A bid of £50 over the trade buyers' maximum can be enough to clinch a car, but always stay within your limit.
- It helps if you know someone who will do a bit of respraying for you or other minor work.
- If you make a mistake, and hate the car you have bought, cut your losses and put it into an auction to dispose of it.
- But you can pick up genuine bargains... like a black Vauxhall Astra just out of warranty that ran impeccably for two years until it was time to go back to an auction for something else.

If you are a window cleaner, teacher or accounts department manager who has plucked up courage to go to your first auction, and you see a car you want, the temptation is to go over your limit to secure it. There is an emotional element for private buyers to suppress, whereas the trade is playing a numbers game, purchasing units if the profit margin seems likely to be right. Dealers have the facilities to correct mechanical problems and this is costed into the forecourt asking price known to be acceptable to buyers.

Auction company staff see expensive emotions grip dads determined to buy a cheap supermini as the first car for their teenage son or daughter. While few women relish this method of buying a car, auctioneers say men sometimes get carried away by machismo. In their refusal to be outdone by a rival male bidder they end up paying more than they need. Remember to act with the professionalism of a trader and only buy when the moment is right for you.

On arrival at an auction, you might for an instant feel life would be simpler visiting a dealer with a choice of 50 used cars, with maybe five of them at roughly the right price. Maybe a little face-to-face dealing is not so daunting after all. Such feelings are understandable because the scale of an auction can be unnerving. The large centres can handle more than 1,000 vehicles in a day and decisions have to be made rapidly once the auction is rolling. On a typical day there will be a mix of cars: low mileage/nearly new, high mileage/ex-fleet, ageing/fading and so on. The owners of the cars could be dealers, finance companies, lease/contract hire firms or private sellers.

It is best to visit an auction at least once before bidding. On the day you intend to buy a car, allow lots of time to acclimatise, read the catalogue, survey the choice and fix your top price on particular cars and your absolute limit. You will be bidding for a car that you and your rival trade or private bidders have not driven. You can inspect the car thoroughly beforehand to gain clues about its condition, but worn mechanical parts will go unseen while you dwell on a minor door scratch.

Provided you have a rough idea as to how much you will pay for body repairs, there is advantage in buying a damaged car. A trader does not want any delays before being able to re-sell it. Time holding slow-selling stock costs money.

The car will be driven into the auction hall. Listen to the sound of the engine as part of your evaluation of the car, then carefully to the auctioneer's description because it is a legally-binding statement. Make a note of what the auctioneer says.

You also need to understand something about cars or have someone with you who does, because many waiting to be sold will have something

## GRAND CONTENDER

### RENAULT CLIO

REN 155

**NEW CAR SAYS...**
FOR Well priced, fun
AGAINST Less-than-robust cabin
SUM UP Still makes sense

**USED** (1998-2001)
**PARKER'S CHOOSER SAYS...**
FOR Space; comfort; value
AGAINST Less fun than the old Clio
VALUE Well equipped; residual values are now slipping as the new 'Collection' line-up devalues

wrong with them. This might be as significant as a suspect transmission or as minor as a damaged sun visor. It could be something far more subtle, such as a popular model with a high mileage or unwelcome exterior paint colour/seat trim combination, which will affect the realistic sale price.

Many cars sold at auctions are the also-rans in the race for used car sales. Franchised dealers keep the best trade-ins to resell, usually through a branded scheme backed by and bearing

## INSIDER DATABASE: THE BIG TWO

BCA Europe sales and
marketing department
01428 607 440
Free 'guide to buying and selling',
with commercial conditions, from
0845 600 6644
www.british-car-auctions.co.uk
(click on 'guide to buying and selling')

Manheim Europe
0870 444 0450
www.manheimeurope.com
(click through auction centres/UK
(list and map)/selected site (phone
number and directions)
(click on 'people, places and sales'
for map and list of locations)

the name of the manufacturer. This acts as a safeguard for buyers but they will be expected to pay more than they would at an auction. Car makers also process and spruce up ex-fleet stock to be sold through their networks. Potential profits on big-selling used models tend to be higher than on the equivalent new car.

The motor trade is becoming more selective because of the glut of used cars following years of high volumes of new car sales. At auctions traders want to buy cars in good condition that are appealing to private buyers, likely to sell quickly, and return a decent profit.

The chances of a real bargain arise if you want, or could tolerate, a car that is unfashionable, in a dull colour, or has been replaced by a new model. In may be worth hunting for makes that are out of favour. In early 2003, these would have included MG Rover, Fiat, Proton and Kia.

But you might do better than that. Trade buyers at a particular auction may lack enthusiasm for a model that is over-supplied and commanding poor prices in showrooms. You could be in a

position to top their best bid, stay within your financial limit and buy a car capable of providing sound personal transport for two years or more. Your ability to take advantage of these factors is dependent on your research but a good starting point is the best-selling cars. Study magazines and price guides to see which cars are losing the most value over their first three years. If many similar cars are in the same auction, you have a strong chance of being able to outbid the trade on the one that takes your eye. For example, look out for a cluster of Renault Clios, Citroen Saxos, Fiat Puntos or Nissan Micras.

Spending your whole budget on an auction car is risky. It is best to keep something in reserve to pay for a full service and to correct any significant faults that may be revealed. If all is well, the money can stay in your savings account. It is also sensible when budgeting to buy a used car, to allow for a warranty to cover faults on major components.

On auction day, you need to be on your toes and ready to bid when your target car comes into the hall. Make an early bid to gain confidence though obviously keep within your budget.

Bids normally add £100 at a time and the auctioneer looks for a raised hand or catalogue. Contrary to popular belief, you will not spend £10,000 on a car you don't want by sneezing or scratching your head. The auctioneer will probably recognise the trade buyers (not all wear sheepskin coats) and will want to ensure private bidders understand the procedure.

If your final bid proves successful, you must head to the rostrum to pay a deposit of around £500 or 10 per cent, whichever is greater. It may be possible to lodge a deposit in advance.

Auction firms are always happy to accept cash or accept payment by a banker's draft (ask your branch to organise it for you). Delta and Switch cards are valid (but not credit cards) and you can pay by cheque. You cannot drive the car away until full payment has been made which means cheques have to clear.

In addition to what is called 'the hammer price', you have to pay a buyer's fee that normally includes VAT of about £50 for each £1,500 paid for the car. Auction houses say this guarantees 'good title' to the car meaning that there is no outstanding hire purchase or credit, the car has not been stolen and is not an insurance write-off. You are guaranteed the odometer (mileage) reading is accurate only if this is announced at the time of sale.

Before going to an auction, check with the company on all their rules about payment and have the means of payment ready. Always check in at the

## GRAND CONTENDER
### RENAULT ESPACE

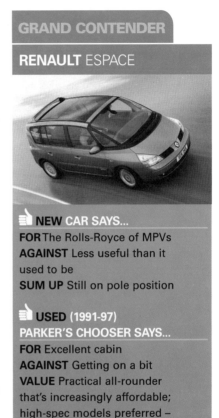

**NEW CAR SAYS...**
**FOR** The Rolls-Royce of MPVs
**AGAINST** Less useful than it used to be
**SUM UP** Still on pole position

**USED** (1991-97)
**PARKER'S CHOOSER SAYS...**
**FOR** Excellent cabin
**AGAINST** Getting on a bit
**VALUE** Practical all-rounder that's increasingly affordable; high-spec models preferred – RN basic by modern standards

office on arrival to confirm auction timings and procedure, and to pay the bidder's premium.

At the moment your bid secures the car, you become responsible for arranging insurance before driving it on public roads. Talk to your insurance company to confirm that temporary cover on an unspecified car to be bought at auction will be extended. Your insurer will want full details as soon as possible. You also have to make sure the car is taxed and, if necessary, has an MoT certificate.

Each car has a reserve price. If the

best bid falls below it, the auctioneer may sell it provisionally subject to the seller's agreement and a refundable deposit will have to be paid. If this amount is not immediately acceptable, the auction house will try to negotiate a price agreeable to both sides.

Cars are auctioned under a series of descriptions according to their condition (see panel). Expect cars over five years old, and those with a purchase price of less than £1,000, to be sold 'as seen and with all their faults'.

There is little chance of going back on the deal once you have bought a car at auction. If the exhaust falls off two miles down the road, the response would be: 'You had a chance to inspect it before buying and check the fixings.' Exhaust systems, tyres, bodywork and interiors are sold 'as seen' and auction companies will not entertain complaints.

People who change their minds make up all sorts of stories including the corniest: 'But my wife doesn't like the colour'. Auction staff are not noted for being softies.

## AUCTIONS

How adventurous  ● ● ● ● ● ● ● ● ● ●
Potential saving  ● ● ● ● ● ● ● ● ● ○

### THE GRAND PLAN

Buying at auction is highly adventurous because you cannot drive the car or have it mechanically checked by an engineer before buying. Sending it back after purchase is rarely an option.
*Tactics:* become familiar with auction procedures before bidding, and stay within your price limit.

**INSIDER GUIDE TO AUCTION HOUSES** *

| | |
|---|---|
| ABERDEEN Scottish Motor Auction Group | 01224 487 000 |
| BIRMINGHAM Birmingham Car Auctions | 0121 749 1331 |
| BRIDLINGTON Bridlington Motor Auctions | 01262 674 044 |
| BLACKBURN East Lancs Motor Auctions | 01254 670 190 |
| CARLISLE Borderway Motor Auctions | 01228 590 990 |
| CHELMSFORD Chelmsford Car Auction | 01245 450 700 |
| CHESTERFIELD Chesterfield Car Auctions | 01246 277 999 |
| CHESTER LE STREET Scottish Motor Auction Group | 0191 410 4243 |
| DALRY Wilson's Auctions | 01294 833 444 |
| DEESIDE Clwyd Auctions | 01244 532 821 |
| DEESIDE Queensferry Motor Auctions | 01244 812 811 |
| DINGWALL Motor Auctions | 020 8684 0138 |
| DONCASTER Bawtry Motor Auctions | 01302 710 333 |
| EDINBURGH Scottish Motor Auctions Group | 0131 443 7163 |
| EASTBOURNE Eastbourne Car Auctions | 01323 520 295 |
| EXETER Exeter Car Auction | 01392 425 481 |
| FERRYHILL Durham County Motor Auction | 01740 650 065 |
| GLASGOW Inter City Motor Auctions | 0141 556 3333 |
| KINROSS Scottish Motor Auction Group | 01577 862 564 |
| LANCING Shoreham Vehicle Auctions | 01903 851 200 |
| LEEDS Motor Auctions Leeds | 0113 277 2644 |
| LEOMINSTER Brightwells Country Vehicle Auctions | 01568 611 325 |
| LIVERPOOL Liverpool Motor Auction | 0151 263 7351 |
| NEWARK Newark Motor Auctions | 01636 671 167 |
| NEWPORT Newport Auctions | 01633 262 626 |
| NORWICH East Anglian Motor Auctions | 01603 409 824 |
| PERTH Inter City Motor Auctions | 01738 623 333 |
| POOLE South Western Vehicle Auctions | 01202 745 466 |
| POULTON-LE-FYLDE West Coast Motor Auctions | 01253 892 488 |
| REDDITCH Arrow Auctions | 01527 510 923 |
| SALTASH Saltash Car Auctions | 01752 841 444 |
| SOUTHAMPTON Southampton Vehicle Auctions | 02380 631 631 |
| TELFORD Telford Motor Auctions | 01952 257 751 |
| WESTBURY Westbury Motor Auction | 01373 827 777 |
| WHITCHURCH Prees Heath Motor Auction | 01948 663 166 |
| WITNEY West Oxfordshire Motor Auction | 01993 774 413 |

* The companies listed are members of the Society of Motor Auctions, a division of the Retail
Motor Industry Federation (01788 538 301); website www.rmif.co.uk

## Chapter 10

# Private sellers

The majority of people are honest but never forget that the rule is: let the buyer beware

"To exert pressure on the price the buyer needs to suppress any sign of excitement about the car"

phone number to call. In theory, private sales are best: why give the profit to the trade when you can keep it for yourself and people should be able to negotiate openly and finalise a private deal over a cup of tea.

If you hate the idea of buying a car from strangers, take comfort from the knowledge they will find the prospect even more stressful. In this, the 10th and final way of buying, the fundamental rule remains the same: many are selling while you want to buy just the one car that's right for you.

Local newspaper small ads are brimming with cars for sale and there are many more available via cards in shop windows. Cars also advertise themselves through messages Sellotaped to vehicle windows offering a price, an encouraging comment and a

It happens all the time, but be aware that the world has plenty of people who want to cheat. This means you must approach a private purchase with caution and a little cunning. Assume the worst, and you should not come unstuck. Anything better will be as pleasant as it is unexpected.

The way you approach making the initial call in response to an ad is crucial. Always say you are calling about 'the car that was advertised'. It is a way of finding out whether this is the private sale you want or whether the ad was placed by a small-time trader posing as a private individual. If the seller has to ask which car you

## DOS AND DON'TS WHEN BUYING PRIVATELY

DO insist on seeing the registration document
DO check the details match the car and the document
DO inspect locks for damage or differences between them which might suggest replacements
DO investigate the car's past
DO arrange for an inspection unless you have real knowledge about cars, or know someone who does
DO walk away unless you are completely happy
DON'T buy on private terms if you suspect the seller is a dealer
DON'T be pressured into buying
DON'T let the owner take the car to you
DON'T be afraid to bargain as many sellers allow for price haggling
DON'T forget the rule: let the buyer beware.

SOURCE: AA

mean, the trader has been rumbled.

We can assume the majority of people are honest, but selling a car tends to bring out the worst in us. After the new owner has driven off, how often do sellers kick themselves for forgetting to mention the poor state of the tread on the spare tyre?

But finding out about that, and anything else wrong with the car, is the responsibility of the buyer. Several

companies will check whether a car is stolen, has outstanding finance owing or is an insurance company write-off. Motoring organisations will provide a detailed report on a used car. Firms offering these services include: www.hpicheck.com (01722 422 422), AA Used Car Data Check (0800 234 999), RAC Vehicle Examinations (0870 533 3660), AA Vehicle Inspection (0800 783 4610).

The seller need only answer questions honestly. Buyers will, of course, neglect to say they liked a car so much they would have gone to their maximum of £4,250 rather than the price of £4,000 that has just been agreed.

After the initial phone call establishes the person has just the one car for sale, you arrange a day and time to inspect it. This should always be at their home or place of work and in daylight so that you can get a good look at the car. It is wise, especially for women, to be accompanied.

You can be sure a private seller wants to be rid of the car as speedily as possible. As the seller's only area of negotiation is price, the buyer is in a strong position, even if 'o.n.o' (or nearest offer) was not specified in the ad. To exert pressure on the price the buyer needs to suppress any sign of excitement about the car. Instead, a silent and exhaustive examination of the car is far more effective. This builds tension over what defects might have been found. It increases the anxiety of the owner who starts to visualise another weekend wasted by potential buyers who don't turn up.

Next, ask some questions such as how long the car has been for sale, the

## INSIDER GUIDE TO PRIVATE CAR SALES

- The value of Britain's used car market in 2001 was £25.4bn (£1.9bn down on the previous year)
- Dealers' sales fell 82,000 to 3.61m while the private-to-private market dipped by 246,000 to 2.57m
- Overall sales of cars up to two years old fell by 97,000 to 937,000 and accounted for 15% of the market
- Sales of cars aged three to five years went down by 118,000 to 1.66m, with the share of the market falling to 26%
- Total sales of cars aged six to eight years rose by 57,000 to 1.35m, pushing the sector's market share up to 21%
- Private-to-private sales in cars aged nine years or more fell by more than half a million over the course of 2000/2001
- Franchised and non-franchised dealers' share of the market reached an all-time high of 57%, up from 51% in 2001

SOURCE: BCA EUROPE USED CAR REPORT 2002

reason for the sale, and what it is being replaced with. Point out excessive wear on seats, marks on the headlining, scratches on the fascia and anything else that might justify offering a lower price. Before making an offer, recap on the details of the car and ask if the owner is certain the mileage shown on the car was correct when bought. Avoid asking whether the mileage is genuine as this implies the owner might have wound the clock back.

If you then make an offer, pitch it far enough below the asking price to try for a substantial saving, but near enough to keep them interested. On a £6,000 car, say: "I like it but I don't want to go much above £5,500." Avoid the temptation to start chatting, look the owner in the eye, and await a response. The offer may be near enough the owner's realistic objective to make an immediate agreement possible.

But it might be too low and the seller will insist that a further £250 is the lowest acceptable figure. The buyer then faces a poker player's dilemma: do you call the buyer's bluff or raise the offer, maybe to a figure halfway between the two? If you reach this point, it should be possible to shake hands on a deal.

When a price is agreed, the next step is to decide on the method of payment. Check on everything to be included, especially if the sale price is subject to the fitting of a new tyre, wing mirror or other item. Some sellers like cash, others fear they might be mugged on the way to the bank. Put the details of the deal in writing and both sign it, each keeping a copy.

Before paying, make sure you see

the car's registration document (it should have a watermark) and check that the name of the present keeper, VIN (vehicle identification number), model and colour of the car are correct. Be sure there is a valid MoT certificate. Also, check the VIN inside the engine compartment and look for any signs of tampering. It is critical to confirm that the car you are buying is genuine.

This is because the worst that can happen can be pretty grim. It could be a 'cut and shut' (the two better halves of two write-offs welded together).

The perfect paintwork might be sparkling but the passenger safety cells could have been weakened and might break up in a crash an undamaged car would comfortably survive.

With motoring and safety organisations spotlighting danger cars like these, it is not surprising that private sales of cars are declining. There are, of course, other reasons, such as the frenetic pace of modern life. Busy people can do without the hassle of answering ads, going to a stranger's home, and ending up with a purchase for which they would have virtually no support in law if it turned out to be a dud.

In 2001, the UK used car market fell by 419,000 units to 6.4m compared with 2000, according to a report by car auctioneers BCA Europe. This, it said, was a result of a weak market for private sales.

This suggests people are holding on to cars longer which is logical given the increase in reliability over the past decade or two. But the real reason, says BCA's Used Car Market 2002 report, is that more buyers are going to dealerships which make a concerted attempt to trade in cars up to eight years old.

The BCA report, based on interviews with 3,000 car users, shows that there were 108 used car sales per thousand people in the UK in 2002. This readiness to trade (by professionals as well as private sellers) was beaten only by Holland (118 per 1,000), a country with a much smaller market. Judging by recent statistics, people in the UK will continue to keep buying used cars with enthusiasm, but they appear to be more comfortable doing so via a third party trader rather than directly.

## PRIVATE SELLERS

How adventurous ●●●●●●●●●●
Potential saving ●●●●●●●●○○

THE GRAND PLAN
There's plenty of adventure here: you're buying from a stranger and have no comeback if the car turns out to be a shocker. Gaining and retaining the psychological upper hand is essential. Tactics: look at many cars, walk away unless convinced the deal is sound.

## INSIDER GUIDE TO CAR INSPECTION

A thorough DIY examination of a used car can save you thousands of pounds by revealing faults that abort a planned purchase. Take this book when you go to view a car and go through the checklist below so the seller knows you are working to a plan. Make notes as the seller watches.

The procedure below is part of how RAC engineers go about a survey. You may not have their knowledge and experience, but you can find obvious faults by following a step-by-step plan, and possibly unnerve the seller sufficiently to admit some of the car's bad points. Challenge the seller on everything you find and seek a lower price.

### BODYWORK

1 Form a general impression and consider whether the car seems genuine

2 Look to see whether the model badge matches the specification on the registration documents

3 Score a minus point if a plastic letter has been added to the model badge. This can be a cheap way of trying to push up the asking price

4 Check whether body panels are consistent, look for evidence of repaired accident damage, and consider whether the colour and texture of the paintwork match all over

5 Run a magnet over the bodywork to show up any dents touched up with body filler

6 Have a look beneath the bonnet and under the boot lid for bad welds, untidy seams or any other evidence of accident repairs

7 Check for rust and paint bubbles, particularly on sills, wheel arches, seams, door bottoms and suspension mountings

### ELECTRICAL

1 Check headlights, dashboard warning lights, and other electrical equipment. Remember repairs to central locking and electric window systems can be expensive. Don't forget to test the obvious: hazard lights, windscreen wipers and horn

2 Test the audio system (radio, stereo and CD player)

### ENGINE

1 Look for oil leaks, and defective or damaged hoses and drive belts. You don't have to be an expert to realise that the general condition of the engine can reveal the degree of care and attention the car has received

2 Check oil and coolants for low levels or any sign of contamination.

3 If the engine is reconditioned, ask for evidence. A bill may be produced but ask to see a warranty

## INTERIOR

1 Safety first. Make sure the seatbelts show no sign of damage or wear, check for loose buckles and faulty mountings

2 Badly worn seats and pedals can suggest high mileage more accurately than an odometer reading, especially if no service history is available

3 Check door, window and sunroof seals for any sign of leaks. Damp patches in the carpet could mean a rusting floor panel

## TEST DRIVE

Be certain you are insured before driving the car. If not, you can learn a lot as a passenger if you follow a plan.

1 Insist that the test drive is long enough to evaluate the car properly. The route should involve a variety of road conditions such as hills, stop-start urban driving, and open roads

2 Listen for odd noises from the engine and suspension

3 Concentrate on the priorities: steering, brakes and clutch. At the end of the test drive, let the engine idle and look under the bonnet for oil or water leaks

## TYRES

1 Include the spare when you check the tyres for tread depth and damage. The grooves of the pattern must be at least 1.6mm throughout a continuous band comprising the central three-quarters of the breadth of the tread and round the entire outer circumference of the tyre

2 If any tyres appear soft, remember under-inflation shortens their life

3 Check for any bulges or cuts in the tyre wall that could lead to a blow-out at speed

## LEGAL RIGHTS ON PRIVATE SALES

· The general rule is 'let the buyer beware'. It is up to the buyer to ask all the questions to determine the history of the car, to inspect it or arrange for an inspection to confirm its condition

· A history check is recommended to avoid difficulties later such as unpaid finance

· The seller must not misdescribe or misrepresent the car

· If the car is described as having one previous owner, but has more, then a claim for compensation might follow

· There is usually little that can be done about a car that has developed a defect after sale unless that sale was prompted by a mis-description

SOURCE: RAC

## Chapter 11

# The right car, the right way

### Decide whether you will love it or respect it

"It's human nature to dream of owning a car that is unsuitable for the tasks you will set it"

We have now examined in some detail the 10 different methods of buying a car. By this point, you should be able to balance risk against potential saving and be ready to narrow the ways of acquiring a car down to two or three. This chapter shows you how to secure the right car in the right way, and, of course, at the right price. Let's assume for a moment you are a first time buyer or hate dealers because of an unhappy experience a couple of years ago. Even if you believe you are the world's worst car buyer, and think everyone is much smarter because of their motoring knowledge, there is nothing to prevent you saving a grand or more.

Self-discipline is essential because seemingly irresistible cars and deals leap out from TV screens, magazines and newspapers and internet websites. There will be plenty of offers to save

£1,000 or more. The words are there in front of you, but are meaningless if the figure is deducted from a retail price the seller knows is unrealistically high. To save the magic grand you have to search until you find the car that is genuinely less than the price you would have paid without exploring at least some of the 10 ways of buying. In the search for a car, you are pitting your wits against clever financiers, imaginative advertising agencies, smooth-talking marketing departments and a host of others who know we all want a bargain.

The starting point, as we have said, should be a franchised dealership where, each day, managers compare sales performance with targets. To succeed, private buyers need to adopt a similarly businesslike approach. That means a determination to avoid being rushed into a purchase and using the advantage of needing only one car. Retail car executives have to sell a certain number of new cars a month, whether it is 10 in a small dealership or thousands in a large motor retail group. To achieve their targets they rely on a sales and marketing programme.

Franchised dealers are invariably under great pressure from manufacturers striving to maintain or increase their share of the UK market. Manufacturers try to create sufficient interest in one of their models to make you at least visit a dealership and sit in the car. But car buyers have changed the rules of the game in recent years by buying a new car in another way, or going for what Rolls-Royce Motor Cars likes to call 'previously owned'. Buyers enjoy a far bigger advantage than most people realise.

First, make sure the timing works to your advantage and allow at least a month for research. The maximum allotted time for a purchase should be three months. Any longer and the process will start to drag and could bounce you into a bad decision. On average, it takes about eight weeks for a purchaser to move from deciding to buy a car to clinching a deal. It is a reasonable period because whether

## VOLKSWAGEN GOLF

**NEW CAR SAYS...**
**FOR** Touchy-feely quality materials
**AGAINST** Suddenly feeling old
**SUM UP** Still the most sensible private choice

**USED (1992-98) PARKER'S CHOOSER SAYS...**
**FOR** Quality, reputation; reliability
**AGAINST** Little chance of finding a bargain
**VALUE** Superior prices for superior cars; few rivals can match Golf's longevity

£500 or £50,000 is at stake, it will be a significant financial commitment based on your means. Most people tend to spend rather more than intended on a car: the purpose of this book is to ensure you spend less than you expected. There are a few basic selection rules that should be followed before moving on to study whether the car is new or used, sourced in the UK or imported. Here, we look at each from the viewpoint of what the buyer wants, and how the trade sees it:

# HOW THE BUYER'S HOPES CLASH
# WITH THE SELLER'S STRATEGY

### INSIDER RULE 1
Only buy a car you respect, like or love

**Buyer's hopes:** if you want a sensible car to get from A to B, are open-minded about the make, not fussy about colour, and might buy new or used, you are in a strong position. There is a huge potential market, and you need think about only the price, equipment and condition/mileage if it is a used model. You can compare the same new model with different equipment packs offered by the manufacturer, and different models that are priced around your budget. But there is a danger in being too pragmatic. It can land you with a car that makes a lot of financial sense, but one you hate. Ford once revamped the Escort (predecessor to the Focus) and produced a 'committee car'. It was easier and cheaper to build than the previous model, and had loads of 'sensible' improvements. The press savaged the car, drivers were unmoved by it and Ford had to inject costly 'personality'. So be warned and do not assume that in time you will begin to enthuse about a car that does not stir you from the start. On the other hand, it's fine if you need only to judge a car on its reliability and view anything more, including actually liking it, as a bonus.

**Seller's strategy:** showroom staff regard the open-minded as weak. They see apparent indecision as an opportunity to direct you towards the car that will make them the fattest profit. You can go along with this as long as you stay strong-willed. Be sure about your list of essential features such as airbags on a used car or a multi-change dashboard CD player on a new one. Be ready for the patter about 'no, it doesn't have that but it does have...'. You will gain showroom credibility and increase the chances of driving a better deal by demonstrating you are not a pushover and specifying your priorities. Do not be in a hurry and show you have researched widely. It's simple really: force them to work hard to sell you a car that you may or may not buy.

## INSIDER RULE 2
### Only buy a car that suits your needs

**Buyer's hopes:** it's human nature to dream of owning a car that is unsuitable for the tasks you will sey it. So be realistic and focus on the sort of car that will do what you need whether it is hatchback or estate; petrol or diesel; sporty or economical. Later, we will look at other key factors. For example, how a low asking price might cost you more later. This is because the value will tumble over the years more quickly than a comparable model which costs more new. You can come to terms with some deviations from perfection, but buying a three-door hatchback when you regularly give a lifts is plain daft.

**Seller's strategy:** being a good salesman entails pointing up the positives and skating over the negatives. Be ready for lines such as 'of course, a five-door is going to cost you more ... this one over here only came in last week and has a fitted...'. Spend more if it is essential, but don't be cajoled into forking out an extra £200 because a car has metallic paint if this isn't your priority.

## INSIDER RULE 3
### Only buy a car you can afford

**Buyer's hopes:** this is a tricky one. You will almost certainly find yourself encouraged to go over budget but don't waver. Fix and never lose sight of the amount you hope will be sufficient to acquire the car you need, and a slightly higher limit that you will not cross, come what may. The way to approach this is explored in more detail in chapter 14 (Set a budget).

**Seller's strategy:** this is as simple for the seller as it is demanding for you. Whenever a dealer suggests a particular car, there is a motive. The reason might be a used car that has hung around for too long. It could be a good buy because, unknown to you, it is destined to go to auction the following day. Test the salesman by making an offer below the stated price. Once the salesman starts to edge up the price, be wary (he'll be thinking of his commission). A dealer, auctioneer, car supermarket or private seller is entitled to gain the greatest reward in a sale, as long as the transaction is carried out legally and honestly.

Manufacturers are obsessed with giving their cars youth appeal even though many people with larger disposal incomes are in their fifties or sixties. It is all to do with the image of the brand or the individual model, and middle-aged people do not want to be categorised in that way. Car selection is driven by many factors and manufacturers spend a lot of money on demographic surveys aimed at discovering what motivates people. Far less money is invested in why people walk out of a showroom without committing themselves. First purchases are normally used models, not least because giving a 17-year-old a new car could create excessive expectations.

**A car change can be triggered for a host of reasons:**

- Higher/lower income
- A better job, less well-paid job, or no job
- Your current car stinging you with a repair bill a month before it's due for an MoT
- Acquiring children or a dog
- Children becoming teenagers and increasing the amount and size of possessions that need moving around
- Divorce followed by renewed interest in sports cars
- New interest that requires more load space such as rock-climbing, surfing or gardening

- The need to pull a caravan or boat
- Retirement, and the desire to drive a smaller car, or a 4x4 to make the most of chances for exploration

The best approach is to make a shortlist of the four or five cars you are considering (new or used) and, without cheating, test them against the following criteria:

- The six types and lengths of journey you expect to make over the next two to three years for work, leisure, holidays and so on. Think about the amount of time you will drive alone or with passengers
- The six features you most want in terms of safety (anti-lock brakes might be top), comfort (air conditioning is increasingly standard on new cars), refinement (ride quality and quietness) and image (brand name, body style etc)
- The cost (insurance, fuel consumption, servicing and repairs) plus the price of borrowed money in monthly repayments. Remember the important but often forgotten issue of depreciation. After three years new cars are worth anything from one-third to two-thirds of their recommended retail price

In the next three chapters, we have a look at the choice of cars, consider car brands and finally set the budget before it's time to make the final choice.

## INSIDER GUIDE TO CAR MAKER JARGON

Car manufacturers see only success. Their business is so competitive they must never let their optimism wane. This is reflected in the way they talk and write. What follows has been taken from marketing documents, and then translated to reveal its more accurate meaning.

- *Price realignment:*
  Prices are rising

- *Model realignment:*
  Derivatives you might have wanted to buy have been axed to save money in production, or they made a mistake and they are not selling

- *More assertive character:*
  A new front bumper and maybe radiator grille

- *State-of-the-art features:*
  Items you would normally expect such as air conditioning and automatic wipers

- *Equipment relevant to everyday needs:*
  What you assume will be on a car

- *Reassuringly cosy:*
  Small cabin

- *Restyled headlamps and rear lights:*
  The cheapest way we could make the car look different in a mid-life revamp

- *Striking headlamps:*
  The sort you see on lots of cars

- *Ultimate accolade:*
  A motoring magazine award

- *Striking elements of design:*
  It may look odd but we had to make it look different

- *Extremely spacious:*
  About average for the class of car

- *Harmonious way the bumper and chrome grille blend into the bonnet:*
  They fit together

## Chapter 12

# Survey the choice

**Purchase in haste, repent at leisure – allow two months to research the market before buying**

*"You should go hunting at the time of year, day of the week and hour of the day when you are least expected"*

Car manufacturers and their dealers aim to capture you in a pincer movement. TV commercials and newspaper/magazine ads are intended to get the purchasing juices flowing and propel you to the showroom where a dealer completes the sale. That is how you are supposed to behave, so be awkward.

You will have in your mind the makes of new car that interest you arranged in some sort of shortlist. Flexibility is strength and needs to be because the sales forces ranged against you are powerful. In the next chapter, we will look at all the main car brands and discuss their virtues or vices. It is likely this appraisal will either support your preferences or prejudices. In this game, staying open-minded is all-important until you, and not the salesman, go for the kill. First, here is a modus operandi for skilful car buying. As we have said, it is best to allow two months for buying a car and perhaps persuading someone to take your present vehicle

as a trade-in. At this point, a quiet but persuasive voice is urging you on to drop in at a local dealership and kick the tyres of the red sports car that caught your eye yesterday. But you purchase in haste, repent at leisure. Do not succumb to the siren voices. Never do the obvious. Avoid becoming showroom fodder.

To beat the car-selling business at its own game, you need to turn the tables on the professionals. You should go hunting at the time of year, day of the week and hour of day when you are least expected. You could start the process in early October with a determination to buy in the first half of

December. That's right, just when you feel you should be preparing for Christmas. But that is precisely the point. Or, you could start researching in the first half of December and go for the jugular during the first couple of weeks of February when dealers are keen to shift stock ahead of the new registration plate on March 1.

You must try to catch sales staff when they are hungry for a sale because that raises your chances of a substantial saving. You cannot barter with your supermarket when buying groceries but you can when buying a car, whether it's new or used. You are expected to go forth in spring when expensive sales and marketing campaigns are geared to your reaction to the feel-good factor that is supposed to come with daffodils, Easter eggs, lighter evenings and a new registration mark. This is a good time if you are looking for a new car and want one of the latest models. If you wait until summer, when holidays take priority over car buying, you will find the deals are more attractive. In late summer, sales efforts gear up for the September 1 plate change. Consider an inexpensive personal number plate that blurs the ageing factor of your cars over the two or three years you keep them as you transfer the plate.

Once located, your car will be one of more than 27 million on the roads of Britain. The car is a commodity and three out of four households have at least one, according to government statistics. Car ownership is far from exclusive, and this makes buying research relatively easy. Among your circle of 20 or 30 relatives and closest

**GRAND CONTENDER**

## CHRYSLER VOYAGER

### NEW CAR SAYS...
**FOR** Big
**AGAINST** The Espace is better
**SUM UP** Putting the 'van' in minivan

### USED (1997-2001)
**PARKER'S CHOOSER SAYS...**
**FOR** Very roomy; loads of equipment
**AGAINST** US-style thirst; poor crash test results
**VALUE** Generous standard equipment; reasonable prices; holding its value quite well.

friends there is likely to be information of value to you. Conversations about buying a new car tend to be limited to the make, colour and whether it should be new or used. You should start probing to find out where other people bought their cars and whether the experience was pleasurable or a nightmare. Manufacturers research your buying experience by conducting surveys among buyers of new cars to evaluate how well the dealer did his job. Your answers to seemingly innocent questions will have a direct bearing on

## GRAND CONTENDER

### FIAT MULTIPLA

**NEW CAR SAYS...**

**FOR** Daring design, good to drive
**AGAINST** Popular prejudice
**SUM UP** People don't know what they're missing

**USED PARKER'S CHOOSER SAYS...**

**FOR** Clever design; good ride
**AGAINST** Looks; width
**VALUE** Clever six-seater compact MPV beats Vauxhall Zafira and Renault Scenic on specification and price.

bonuses paid to the dealership. Your own research might identify a dealership that has intelligently looked after the interests of people in your research group, or performed consistently badly. In all retail experiences, we should seek clarity, honesty and the additional effort that turns the routine into something a little better, or resolves a problem without fuss. Do not rely on your memory during these important weeks of research because you are going to come across a mass of information, phone numbers and website addresses.

You should also keep a list of the car retailers you have visited and make a note of your reactions to the level of service offered. Keep newspaper ads you have scanned and hold on to motoring magazines or road tests. Make it an early priority to tour your local franchised dealers but only go to those selling models within your price range. If your new car must have a maximum list price of £10,000 there is little point in wasting time in BMW showrooms. Before developing a plan of action, it is important to acclimatise to motor trade territory. People who buy in other sectors (clothes especially) often get a buzz from the experience but many feel intimidated in car showrooms. They are preparing to make a major financial commitment and plenty of people will have filled their minds with the notion that 'you'll be ripped off'. That is not necessarily so, but you have to work hard to land the best deal and always need to be wary.

Walk into the showroom and look at the cars. Perhaps you have no intention of buying during this early reconnaissance but note how the showroom staff treat you. The chances are you will be pounced on or ignored, so get used to it. A courteous enquiry after a few minutes is worth noting and means the dealership is worth a return visit. Sales staff should never let you walk out without having a word, but it happens.

After looking around the latest coupe, or sitting in the modern version of your four-year-old hatchback, you will start believing that, somehow, you must afford a new car. Before leaving the dealership, pick up a brochure about the cars that interest you and be sure to take a price list (it will probably be a separate sheet).

Then look at the dealer's used models. They will seem far less inviting, not least because they are lined up in a row in the wind and rain. Force yourself to keep used cars on your agenda because of the potential savings. Make notes about the used cars: '99V Ford Focus 2.0 Ghia, 55,000 miles, £7,750 ... unmarked outside but stain on rear seat upholstery. CD standard?'

This way, you are beginning to analyse and evaluate rather than relying on instinct. There is a way to go yet before making a decision on the model of car, new or used, and the way you buy. The more detailed your research from the beginning, the greater will be your invaluable database, and the quicker your confidence will grow.

Next, visit a used car superstore where you will experience the motoring equivalent of a large electrical goods store. There will be lots of choice, and stock is arranged in a way that makes comparisons easy (see chapter 3). And test the other eight of the 10 methods that hold out any appeal to you. No country has a wider choice of makes and versions of new cars than the UK. There is everything from city cars to luxury limousines. Most will appeal to some buyers, while all have limitations or disadvantages. We will also examine industry thinking to help you deal with marketing patter. Some of the cars mentioned are no longer made. Our objective is to look at new and used models in this class of car, so you can decide which one is for you.

## Mini cars

'Small but perfectly formed' ... you know the saying, but often it does not apply among mini cars (not to be confused with the obsolete 1959 Mini or its successor, BMW Group's MINI). The main attraction, whether new or used, is cheapness. With cars, price structures often do not relate to length, width and height as there are plenty of beautifully engineered European coupes costing a lot more than budget-priced large saloons from Asia. But mini cars are, in the main, offered fresh from the assembly line for less than £10,000. The production plants are often in Asia or eastern Europe where costs and retail prices are low, people earn less than in Britain and there is a demand for basic cars. A bargain in Britain, you might say, but it depends on your definition. This is a mass market and the low prices make it hard for retailers to make a good profit. You will find it interesting to compare the Suzuki Wagon R+ and the Vauxhall Agila because they are essentially the same car. Japanese Suzuki and General Motors (Vauxhall in Britain) shared the development costs.

Wagon R/Agila are typical of the species: low asking price new, and inexpensive to service and insure. They have reasonable interior space for the money but are fairly basic in all departments and the boot is tiny. They are quite capable of completing 300-mile journeys but it is a tiring experience. They score better as an easily-parked, second car for city people with access to a bigger car for even medium-size loads. Do not confuse lightness of body with weakness because these little cars can be tough. South Korea's Daewoo Matiz and Hyundai Atoz are among the pick of the selection for people who demand no more than a means of getting around. (The Hyundai's name stands for A to Z). The VW Lupo and its less expensive relative, the Seat Arosa, feel more like proper cars. The MCC Smart, made by the same group as Mercedes-Benz, is a current fashion icon, but you may find its looks too odd for your taste.

### MINICAR CHECKLIST

Be sure you won't feel too vulnerable, think about whether your usual passengers will fit in it, and decide whether the lack of load space will be tiresome.

## Superminis

Big sellers like the Ford Fiesta, Vauxhall Corsa and VW Polo dominate this class. They sell mainly to private customers, known in the trade as retail buyers. These are people spending their own money rather than being provided with a fleet car, or running one as part of their business. Supermini buyers have made the trade sit up over the past decade with their greater knowledge, determination to get more for their money and brand promiscuity. They switch from Ford to Toyota if it suits them, and vice-versa. Do not waste the good work done by earlier buyers and be sure you make someone work hard for the sale. Forget individuality unless you want to send the purchase bill soaring by going for a hot derivative. This will involve more outlay, higher insurance premiums, costlier servicing and bigger fuel bills.

With any car you get the best value by choosing the most basic version of a model that is also available with a high-performance engine. That is because the low-profile 1.2-litre car has the same basic engineering that makes it possible for the manufacturer to fit a 2.0-litre engine with some adaptations to the suspension plus different wheels and tyres. Making key decisions is essential with superminis because the choice is so wide. A typical shortlist may well include the Ford Fiesta, a big seller praised in road tests, and the VW Polo which remains appealingly dependable. But also take a look at newcomers like the Honda Jazz which is well built and has rear seats with a clever folding mechanism. However, you do not get the same choice of engines and equipment levels as you do with the Vauxhall Corsa. The Skoda Fabia (its Volkswagen Group engineering is in part shared with the VW Polo) could be the one for you, once the MINI (with its strong personality) has been ruled out as a 'maybe next time' dream. The French have strong contenders including the Peugeot 106 and 206, Citroen C3 and Saxo and Renault Clio.

### SUPER MINI CHECKLIST

Think about the balance between performance and running costs; cabin space (especially rear legroom) and load area (plus ease or otherwise of folding hatchback seats); quality of fascia and other plastic mouldings; the feel and durability of the seat upholstery; length of warranty, insurance costs and service intervals.

## Small family cars

The choice of small family cars used to be basically between hatchbacks or saloons, but the range has become much more interesting and the body styles more varied. You can have a small car with a Mercedes (A-class) or Audi (2 or 3) badge, too, which brings to the fore another important facet of car buying. Over the past five years, companies running fleets of cars for employees have become increasingly interested in 'whole life costs'. In other words, a car that costs 20 per cent less than another similar model can prove more expensive over three years because of servicing, fuel and insurance bills and, crucially, depreciation. So, in this class, the Mercedes and Audi are initially pricier than the rest but hold their second-hand values well. This is in part because they are so well built, with high-quality components such as gearboxes, but the value of the badge is also important. The A2 is likely to hold half its selling price over 36 months/36,000 miles which is only a little better than a Ford Focus. But the additional pleasure of driving an A2 and the status of having an Audi parked outside your home has also to be taken in account. Heavyweight performers in this category include the VW Golf and closely-related Audi A3, Renault Megane, Peugeot 307 and Toyota Civic.

In engineering terms, the latest versions of these models are at least on level terms with luxury cars of a decade ago. Costing less, and therefore not offering the same quality, are cars like the Daewoo Lanos, Hyundai Accent and Proton Satria. Likely buyers are older motorists who are content to stay within the speed limit and are past the Nike-moment in their lives when it seems essential to spend more to be seen to be cool. Drive a Focus and an Accent – compare a Golf and a Satria – and you quickly get the idea. The Lanos is best bought new, so you take advantage of the aftersales service, while the Polo is always going to be a good bet on the used car scene. As a basic rule, each new car model is better than its predecessor because the industry continues to make rapid progress. But there are disappointments. Peugeot had to mount a costly marketing campaign to promote the 307 model after it had been judged too expensive for the limited strides it had taken since the 306, the car it had replaced and which was somewhat ahead of its time. The moral of the story is not to allow a salesman to persuade you that this year's model is obviously a lot better than last year's. Ask them to prove it.

### SMALL FAMILY CAR CHECKLIST

There is always a brand new or upgraded version of at least one of these models just on the market, or about to appear, because competition is so intense. Base your choice on brand value, purchase price, whole life costs and expenditure on insurance, fuel etc.

## Medium cars

We are now entering mainstream fleet territory. Models include the Ford Mondeo, Vauxhall Vectra, Renault Laguna, Skoda Octavia and Toyota Avensis. They are sold in vast quantities to leasing and contract hire companies that supply firms needing to keep directors, managers and other staff on the move. Company car drivers become more selective each year and manufacturers must either offer a class act (BMW 3 Series), a great all-rounder (Ford Mondeo) or a compelling financial deal because a particular model fails to set pulses racing (Citroen C5). As with small family cars, you need to weigh prestige (Mercedes C-Class) against the savings available with a volume manufacturer's equivalent that has some originality, such as the Nissan Primera. In this category, it is especially important to think about detail. Compare the superior seats fitted to the Saab 9-3 to the disappointing set in the Peugeot 406. Be clear about whether you want the fluid power of a six-cylinder, turbocharged petrol engine, or the economy of a diesel. Study a brochure, and you will be impressed by the variety of derivatives. However, manufacturers concentrate their sales and marketing efforts on a particular derivative such as '2.0-litre with air conditioning and alloys' at a price ending in '£999'. Stick out for a deal on that one because there are likely to be plenty around. If a particular shade of metallic paint is essential to your needs, combined with an optional extras pack, you will almost certainly have to wait for it and your negotiating stance is weakened.

If you are buying used, remember a flood of cars enters the market each year as, to use industry jargon, they are 'de-fleeted'. Do not let anyone persuade you that these cars should be avoided due to high mileages and perhaps being 'thrashed' by the user. Fleet cars spend a good deal of their life doing an unstressed 80mph on motorways and are regularly and properly serviced. Employers insist on their staff being mobile and contract hire companies have to go to the additional expense of providing replacements if a car is off the road. There are rich pickings here as long as you spend some time finding the right colour (important, when the car is everywhere) and refuse to pay over the odds. If in any doubt, walk away from the deal: there will always be plenty more. For more detail, see chapter 7.

## MEDIUM CARS CHECKLIST

Beware the seductive influence of a posh badge as it can cost you a lot. Think about the boredom factor in the models with poor dynamics. Take care not to make the wrong decision if you are shopping in the large volume middle ground.

## Executive/luxury cars

Executive homes, executive cars ... the adjective is losing its appeal. As superminis and medium cars get bigger, better equipped and more refined, there has to be a good reason to opt for a new executive car. A family that includes three teenagers could be the reason, although that, too, depends how often you transport them together. Then, of course, there is the status factor. Some people, such as senior company directors, may feel compelled to be seen in a Mercedes because lower ranks are driving a Ford or a VW. Most executive cars are run as a business expense, either by a senior manager, someone self-employed , or a partner in a business.

You would, of course, be foolish to reject the chance of running a BMW 5 Series on the firm if offered as part of your employment package. But this sector has changed dramatically with the introduction of company car tax charges based on the cleanliness or otherwise of the exhaust fumes. BMW and Mercedes are the most desirable executive cars, followed by a pack that includes Audi and Jaguar. The Japanese may have taught the world how to build low-to medium-priced cars with consistent quality control, but the Germans retain their grip in terms of delivering a quality experience over three years to high-mileage, hard-working company drivers. Lexus, a new brand of car created by Toyota more than 10 years ago, is regarded as highly by some as the German trio of Mercedes, BMW and Audi. These makes, together with Jaguar, are increasing volume in response to economic pressures. But the drive to reduce the cost of each car through high volumes of production is potentially damaging to any brand. A genuine Rolex watch cannot be bought for £19.99. If it could, those paying hundreds or thousands of pounds for one would switch to another make. If it is size you are after, there are keenly priced options like the Skoda Superb, Hyundai Sonata, Daewoo Leganza and Kia Magentis. You would not see a sales director used to a BMW driving one, even if the Chancellor agreed to waive the company tax bill. They offer lots of room and electrical gadgets, but lack both character and driver pleasure. The executive class can make most sense for those who still prefer an estate car rather than an MPV, the multi-purpose vehicle, also still known by some as a people carrier. For used car buyers, this category makes a lot of sense. Depreciation is heavy on many of the new models and those run by companies still have much to offer after three years and 60,000 miles. Repairs tend to be expensive, and big petrol engines have a mighty thirst, but if they are well looked after (and typical weekly mileage is low) they can continue to serve their driver well.

### EXECUTIVE CAR CHECKLIST

Better bought used than new, if it is your own money being used. An ageing quality car is more likely to please than a more recent inferior one.

## Sports cars

You should by now be picking up the drift of this book and, if a convertible appeals, resolve to buy it any time from late summer through to early February. Buy when the market least expects it and when dealers want to clear stock. Recent mild winters have lengthened the cabriolet season, so there will always be a demand. True devotees of open-air motoring enjoy it throughout the year but deals are always more difficult when the weather is warm and demand strongest. Coupes find buyers anytime, like any other car with a sealed top. People buy sports cars to drive them hard and that makes it essential to check the cost of insurance before you get too excited about the idea. Make sure the folding mechanism of convertibles' hoods works properly. This part of the market is divided between what the industry likes to call the 'affordable' and the pricier exclusive models. But sports cars have a cachet and rarely justify their price based on performance alone. Sporty saloons and hatchbacks can be a better buy if that is your priority. There is nothing quite like driving with the hood down on a soft summer evening, whether you are connecting with the atmosphere of city streets or the sweet smells of the countryside. Cars like the Audi TT are pretty, but expensive. They share much found in a VW Golf. Thoroughbreds like the Porsche Boxster make more sense. The Alfa Romeo GTV (coupe) and Spyder (convertible) are cars to fall in love with. Mercedes-Benz is clever with the mechanical folding hard-top of the SLK. BMW is happy to leave it to owners to decide whether the Z3 is a real sports car or a driver statement. Be clear on which you want your car to be. The Hyundai Coupe from South Korea is a cracking drive for the money but may make the wrong status statement for you. Do not ignore the Japanese contenders because Toyota's MR2 and Celica should be in the frame, whether new or used.

### SPORTSCAR CHECKLIST

Never let the heart rule the head in this sector.

## 4x4s

The arrival of the Porsche Cayenne provides a fillip for the 4x4 market in the UK. Posh Porsche takes on the BMW X5, Range Rover and Mercedes-Benz M-Class among the wealthy who want to pull boats or horseboxes, or simply make a statement. Britain's Land Rover and America's Jeep are the oldest 4x4 marques but many brands offer drivers the chance to get a better grip. You need to do the same with your wallet and senses when shopping in this sector. Prices can be as steep as the hills the vehicles can scale and that is part of the point. Are your weekend destinations sufficiently difficult to reach to justify all-wheel drive? The kit to enable you to go 4x4 is heavy and extra weight brings the need for extra fuel. The Americans call them SUVs (sports utility vehicles) and the term is finding favour here. The last thing manufacturers want is to battle to sell a product with an agricultural image. They prefer to perpetuate 'lifestyle' and advertisements have depicted Land Rovers wading with hippos and Jeeps clambering over boulders in the Rockies. The popular jibe levelled against 4x4s is that they only go off-road when half-parked on a pavement. But they do provide all-weather traction, big load areas on the full-size models and safety aids in the form of a high driving position and rugged construction.

Serious image-building from your SUV comes at a price. Plenty of people feel both more secure and out of the motoring rut in one of the mid-priced models such as the Land Rover Freelander or Honda CR-V.

### 4X4 CHECKLIST

Before you start, decide whether your priority is safety, practicality, or image.

## MPVs

MPVs (multi-purpose vehicles, also known as people carriers) sell massively in the US where they are known as minivans. Some are glorified vans. Surprisingly, the Mercedes V-class is one of the least effective in disguising its pedigree. Unlike 4x4s, MPVs make sense for most people. Seats are higher than in the estate they are replacing. Children love the view and the driver can see further ahead, an important aid to safety. The description 'multi-purpose' derives from seats that swivel to face the rear, fold flat to become tables, lift out, or tumble into the floor as they do so cleverly in the Vauxhall Zafira.

MPVs mark the start of a new era in the motor industry where manufacturers are starting to play with a range of fresh ideas. Virtually all new cars are now assumed to be safe, secure and play CDs to cheer a journey fraught with traffic jams and speed cameras. Designers wrestling with the constraints of interior space and safety legislation tended to make MPVs all look much the same. Sales departments hate that, because it is easier to sell something that is unique or, at least, distinctive. For buyers, it is good news. The Ford Galaxy, VW Sharan and Seat Alhambra are closely related, which allows you to play off one potential purchase against another. The other MPV cloned family comprises the Fiat Ulysse, Peugeot 807 and Citroen C8. The Renault Scenic and Citroen Xsara Picasso are potentially good used buys because the French rivals have grabbed market share with incentives and there are plenty around. The Chrysler PT Cruiser is a sort of MPV but this takes us back to the 4x4 debate: buy it for image but go for a Scenic or Zafira if you want a real MPV.

### MPV CHECKLIST

Be sure you will need to lift out rear seats, otherwise go for an estate if loadspace is a priority. Remember the clones, remind retailers this is a lookalike market and go in hard for a bargain price.

### GRAND CONTENDER

### HYUNDAI SANTA FE

#### NEW CAR SAYS...

**FOR** Porsche-designed powertrain
**AGAINST** Genetically modified look
**SUM UP** Restyled out of contention

#### USED PARKER'S CHOOSER SAYS...

**FOR** Well equipped; easy to drive
**AGAINST** Thirsty petrol engines; odd styling; poor gearchange
**VALUE** A Discovery-sized 4x4 for Freelander money; overall package very tempting; future residual values are only average

## Chapter 13

# Buy the right brand

### Manufacturers are eyeing parts of the market that used to belong to others

"Cars carry an influence far beyond their ability to transport people comfortably and safely. They have come to be seen as part of our identity"

Answer this instinctively. Would you rather have a BMW or a Proton on your driveway? Own a Jaguar or an Audi? Drive a Ford or a Peugeot? You are supposed to find those three questions progressively more difficult to answer. We are dealing with perceptions here, fashion fads, susceptibility to marketing, the male versus female perspective and the difference between the aspirational and the pragmatic. There are no fixed rules, and you are allowed to go against the flow. Indeed, it can be in your financial interests to do so.

However, you will find that prices of new cars, and the value they manage to retain, are directly influenced by the perceived value of a brand. That is the purpose of this insider's guide to the standing of each brand of new car, and a pointer to whether the manufacturer is on the rise or on the decline. Manufacturers spend hundreds of millions of pounds developing an all-new model. They then dig deep again to finance a marketing programme to persuade people to buy the car. Drivers used to be influenced by the preferences of their parents but are now far more fickle. They hunt the bargain, but want the image, and that is why manufacturers keep looking for the perfect balance between volume sales and models that enhance the brand. Ford achieved this brilliantly with the Puma, a little sports car based on the mass-selling Fiesta. The company paid the family of the late Steve McQueen – an actor who became an icon of cool – for the privilege of using his star image in a TV commercial. It gave the impression that McQueen, the quiet action man, was driving a Puma through the streets of San Francisco, the setting for his cult movie *Bullitt* and its memorable car chase. More recently, Citroen negotiated an agreement with the family of the late Pablo Picasso for his name to adorn the manufacturer's MPV (multi-purpose vehicle). The car is unlikely to have been so successful if sold as the Citroen Xsara MPV. The Picasso is one of a number of so-called 'lifestyle' cars. In essence this means they have useful features such as adaptable seats and, not before time, a selection of storage places for oddments. Ford is striving to raise its profile in an effort to sell more cars for more money. Citroen is trying hard to regain its former persona as a well-engineered, slightly quirky marque after previous managements had foolishly turned its cars into re-badged Peugeots (they are part of the same group) in a short-sighted push for sales.

As manufacturers have become more imaginative in design, some have eyed parts of the market that used to belong to others. Mercedes-Benz ventured down market (some would say disastrously with the A-class) while Ford and Vauxhall have headed in the opposite direction with desirable cabriolets such as the Streetka and VX220.

Two trends running in parallel for the past two decades influence every purchase and every sale of a car, new and used, anywhere in the world. First, is the phenomenal increase in the reliability, safety and refinement of cars, thanks to the efforts of the manufacturers. They take great quantities of parts from outside suppliers, channel them to a team of people and robots and produce

## GRAND CONTENDER

## JAGUAR XJ SERIES

### NEW CAR SAYS...
**FOR** Hi-tech alloy construction
**AGAINST** Looks identical to its steel predecessor
**SUM UP** A truly modern classic

### USED (1994 - 2003)
**PARKER'S CHOOSER SAYS...**
**FOR** Massive power; deluxe comfort
**AGAINST** Punishing running costs
**VALUE** Years of refinement have brought the XJ to perfect pitch; all models have every refinement

personal transport that can endure bad treatment for years and still perform reliably for its driver. This is repeated millions of times and, in its own way, is as exciting an engineering feat as landing men on the Moon. The second trend is the way people have demanded more choice, better quality, lower prices and quicker delivery. New cars are far cheaper now than they were in the 1980s in terms of inflation-related prices and value including features from CD players to electronic stability controls.

Once technical advances and broadly increasing wealth are put together, brand value becomes significant.

Brands are fundamental to the consumer. You may well buy Coca-Cola or Pepsi rather than supermarket-branded cola partly because others are likely to see the can or bottle. And perhaps your tonic water, mixed with gin out of sight of your guests, bears the supermarket label. Cars carry an influence far beyond their ability to transport people comfortably and safely. They have come to be seen as part of our identity. Journalists regularly driving the latest new cars know how reactions to them differ when they are in a Porsche one week, and a Kia the next. There could scarcely be a greater contrast. But the differences become less obvious when comparing a Vauxhall with a Toyota, or a Citroen with a Nissan. The perception of cars was once based for many on 'British or foreign' or 'luxury versus popular'. Now, the 1980s music track played over a TV commercial, product placement in a James Bond movie, or association with a celebrity are three of the main factors influencing car buyers. Buyers are also more price-sensitive than ever. They might see one special offer as making a car they would like become easier to afford while another might be seen as making it appear 'cheap and nasty'. It all comes down to brand.

## GRAND CONTENDER

### KIA SEDONA

#### ▣ NEW CAR SAYS...

**FOR** Big, huge, ginormous
**AGAINST** Like steering an ocean liner
**SUM UP** Unbeatable value

#### ▣ USED PARKER'S CHOOSER SAYS...

**FOR** Comfort; value for money
**AGAINST** Indifferent build quality; heavy depreciation
**VALUE** Masses of space and equipment at very tempting prices; depreciation is turning out to be fairly steep, so it's most sensible to buy a used example

# BRANDS TO BUY, BRANDS TO AVOID

The star-rated brand value (from one to five) is an evaluation of prospects for 2004-06. The more powerful the brand image, the better the chances of cars holding their value. Beware models that are rogue intruders such as the van-based V-class, a disaster in the otherwise impressive Mercedes range.

## AC:
specialist sports car for wealthy enthusiasts – buy it if exclusivity excites you (and if you can).
Brand value: * * *

## ALFA ROMEO:
the acceptable face of Fiat Auto (see Fiat below), cast as the Italian equivalent to BMW. Values hold up above average. Fiat UK has encouraged separate Alfa outlets to distance it from the Fiat image. Alfa's future looks bright whatever happens to the Fiat brand.
Brand value: * * *

## ASTON MARTIN:
should do well as long as people flock to Bond movies. Owned by Ford, kept well away from 'blue oval' showrooms, and will remain well above Jaguar in the group pecking order.
Brand value: * * * *

## AUDI:
for years has been trying to match German rivals Mercedes-Benz and BMW in terms of brand value. Audis used to be re-badged VWs but are now sold in distinctive dealerships with lots of smart aluminium. Like the VW brand, Audi is part of the Volkswagen Group headed by former BMW chairman Bernd Pischetsrieder who is passionate about surpassing BMW, the group that ousted him.
Brand value: * * *

## BENTLEY:
a brand with a thrilling future, now part of the Volkswagen Group (like keenly priced Skoda). Future models will be pitched against BMW, which owns the Rolls-Royce brand. Both will be up against the Maybach (see below).
Brand value: * * * * *

## BMW:
this is the brand dealers without it would most like to have in their showrooms, according to trade surveys. With great engines and marketing to match, BMW will continue to prosper which means strong demand for its cars secondhand, so values will be held. Main danger to BMW is the temptation to make its entry price so low it can compete against Ford and other similar makes.
Brand value: * * * *

## BRISTOL:

eccentric automotive offshoot of the company's executive aircraft. If you can't afford your own plane, you can pay as little as £140,000 or so for one of the cars. You've probably never seen a Bristol car. Production volumes are tiny.
Brand value: * *

## CATERHAM:

represents pure driving pleasure. Fans become hooked and love the way these zesty two-seaters hug the road and their value. Caterham is one of a brave bunch of manufacturers continuing the great British tradition of individual sports cars for enthusiasts who don't want a hatchback dressed as a convertible.
Brand value: * * *

## CHRYSLER:

the weakest link in the DaimlerChrysler empire (the company owning Mercedes-Benz acquired the American manufacturer). Chrysler crosses the Atlantic with less conviction than its sister brand Jeep and the 'all-American' retro-styled PT Cruiser is made in Mexico.
Brand value: * *

## DAEWOO:

a victim of the time one of the Asian 'tiger' economies lost its tail. South Korea boasted that its car manufacturers would conquer the world. Daewoo, with its tail between its legs, capitulated and was forced to allow General Motors (Vauxhall in the UK) to acquire it. Model brand value is zilch. Buy it for the after sales service.
Brand value: *

## DAIHATSU:

an odd mix of models, ranging from the neat YRV to the depressing Fourtrak. Daihatsu has no obvious model policy and tries to stretch in too many directions. Buy only if the deal makes sense.
Brand value: * *

## FERRARI:

breathtaking to drive, fabulous racing heritage, lusted after by the top celebrities ... you really don't want to hear any more. The jewel in Fiat's tarnished crown, so valuable it is managed outside Fiat Auto.
Brand rating: * * * * *

## FIAT:

Fiat entered 2003 with mounting debts and Stilo, its latest model, failing to sell as well as hoped. Fiat is the motor industry's Marks & Spencer: it failed to see how the opposition was improving. It relied on domination of its home market while VW etc had other ideas. General Motors, the world's biggest vehicle maker, has a stake in Fiat: the logic of owning the Italian group is not immediately obvious.
Brand value: * *

## FORD:

seems to have been the UK new car market leader for ever and, despite denials, will do what is necessary to stay No 1. Still trying hard to shed the Cortina image that comes with its 'blue oval' badge which is one reason it bought Jaguar more than a decade ago. Now builds no cars in Britain. Fiesta, Focus and Mondeo, its three big sellers, are all fine cars.
Brand value: * * *

## HONDA:

this is a brand on the up. Hard to believe it was once so desperate for sales in Europe it needed to team up with Rover. Now, Honda is starting to seem like a European brand and confidence is rising. A mixed bag of models that includes the bright little Jazz.
Brand value: * * * *

## HYUNDAI:

a stronger survivor than Daewoo from the Korean economic catastrophe, it also controls Kia. Hyundai's brand prospects should slowly rise because its Coupe has to be taken seriously and that is a good omen.
Brand value: * * *

## ISUZU:

not-so-super Trooper is its sole model in the UK. Agricultural, dependable, old-fashioned and strictly for the minority who want an off-roader plough through mud.
Brand value: * *

## JAGUAR:

one of the most fascinating brands. As English as an American-owned car maker can be. The X-type takes on the fabled BMW 3 Series but has family ties with the Ford Mondeo. Jaguar is a good long-term prospect to come through its tricky brand-stretching exercise because it can take on Porsche with the XK8. And Ford Motor Company just has to make the brand work somehow.
Brand value: * * * *

## JEEP:

relies heavily on its all-American heritage. Jeep and the Land Rover are the 4x4 makers with a depth of history but DaimlerChrysler is slow to replace the ancient Wrangler (an adaptation of the original World War II Jeep). Great brand potential but prospects uncertain. The Grand Cherokee is made in Austria for the European market.
Brand value: * * *

## KIA:

now part of Hyundai and posing the group's biggest challenge. Kia has too many models on sale in the UK, and no good ones. Claims it will become Hyundai's 'sporty' sub-brand are laughable. Best bet is the Carens, a cheap way into the fashionable mid-size MPV market if you don't mind driving a poor person's Renault Scenic.
Brand value: *

## LAMBORGHINI:

more rarified than Ferrari, even more manly. You buy the Lambo Murcielago if you have wealth and something to prove.
Brand value: * * * *

## LAND ROVER:

Ford dumped Jacques Nasser, its boss who was shrewd enough to buy Land Rover. History is likely to honour his vision. Heavy investment is showing in the model line-up and all that is good about the Range Rover should cascade down the range.
Brand value: * * * *

## LEXUS:

Toyota's posh-car sub-brand was at first ultra-refined and ultra-dull, but Lexus has acquired an image that is both modern and represents quality.
Brand value: * * * *

## LOTUS:

its future brand strength is based heavily on the appeal of the replacement for the Elise, in 2004/05. Malaysian-owned, so not as British as, say, Caterham or Morgan, but a brand with international appeal.
Brand value: * * * *

## MAYBACH:

DaimlerChrysler is pitching against BMW-owned Rolls-Royce and Volkswagen-owned Bentley with the Maybach, a super-luxurious Mercedes adorned with a resurrected brand of some standing. Expensive and strictly for those who live in castles and penthouses.
Brand value: * * * *

## MAZDA:

a member of the Ford family. For too long, Mazda has been over-dependent on the adorable MX-5, Japan's vision of what a small British two-seater convertible should be. Mazda 6 marked the start of Ford's ambition to make the brand a sort of budget-priced Jaguar. One to watch.
Brand strength: * * *

## MERCEDES-BENZ:

the manufacturer became the motor trade's villain by trying to give all its UK dealers 12 months notice. Dealers fought hard and won better exit deals. Mercedes now has what it wants: a retail network it controls directly in major urban areas and will build brand centres in key areas. Mercedes plays rough, but owners love it. Great range, apart from the V-class (horrid large MPV) and prospects are excellent.
Brand value: * * * * *

## MG:

MG Rover is the car manufacturer even the opposition wishes well, probably because it faces such a struggle to succeed. BMW sold Rover for a tenner and you could say that makes this book seem expensive. MG Rover must replace ageing models and continue the MG-isation of Rover. So far, so good. MG versions of the Rover range are better than the originals.

Brand value: * * *

## MINI:

BMW has brilliantly blended the driving characteristics of a hugely loved little car born in 1959 with its tremendous engineering abilities. The result is a distinctive small car that promises to hold on to two-thirds of its value after three years/36,000 miles.

Brand value: * * * * *

## MITSUBISHI:

Mitsubishi failed to build on its reputation as a 'Japanese BMW' and relied too heavily in the UK on the Shogun 4x4. The naming of Carisma was a woeful mistake as the one thing it lacked was charisma. It is built in Holland but is far less European than a Honda from Swindon. Brand standing, and therefore ability to hold value, is questionable.

Brand value: * *

## MORGAN:

only you can decide it is worth the wait of two to three years for Morgan's traditional 4/4 or the aluminium Aero 8, new, bravely-bold in its styling and BMW-powered. Hangs on to value well because of demand.

Brand value: * * * *

## NISSAN:

Renault took a share in the company and shook Nissan out of its inward-looking ways. The model range has not yet felt the full benefit of the more imaginative European approach, so medium- to long-term prospects are tied in with Renault's (see below). Individual models have more brand value than Nissan itself.

Brand value: * * *

## PERODUA:

this is the poor person's Proton, and Malaysia's No 2 marque. The omens are not good. The Kelisa and Kenari have cheapness as their only virtues and strongly support the case for buying used rather than new.

Brand value: *

## PEUGEOT:

heavyweight players in the brand game. Peugeot research suggests the make is regarded as a cut above, say, Vauxhall. It aspires to be an aspirational manufacturer, but Peugeot lacks Renault's resolve and courage in terms of design. Unlikely to whizz upmarket.

Brand value: * * *

## PORSCHE:

the 911 is one of the great motoring icons, adored by 'real drivers' (the racing professionals and, yes, the wannabes). The Boxster costs less and is also a thoroughbred.

Brand value: * * * *

## PROTON:

brand-challenged, that's Proton. Weird names like Wira don't help models based on obsolete Mitsubishis. Its virtues are low sticker prices (but beware how Protons shed value) and a link through ownership with Lotus.
Brand value: *

## RENAULT:

like the Japanese (it has a managing alliance with Nissan), the French heavyweight is playing the long game. Vel Satis may look weird/gorgeous (delete as necessary) but, whatever your view, it makes Peugeot look dull. A daring design strategy, outcome uncertain.
Brand value: * * *

## ROLLS-ROYCE:

the most illustrious British car brand now goes on cars made by German BMW. A repeat of BMW's success with the MINI is on the cards though on a far smaller scale.
Brand value: * * * * *

## ROVER:

a host of British motoring marques (Austin, Triumph, Rover, Morris and the rest) eventually filtered down into one: Rover. Under-investment and unimaginative management led to brief ownership by BMW, which realised the error of its ways. At MG Rover, the initials MG represent the future and

that means Rover's brand value is poor.
Brand value: *

## SAAB:

part of the General Motors empire. People buy Saabs because they are classless but have an aura of being a cut above most of the opposition. Saab motor show concept cars suggest the brand should get stronger.
Brand value: * * * *

## SEAT:

as Spanish as a German car manufacturer can be. SEAT provides the Mediterranean warmth in the countries of southern Europe for the Volkswagen Group. Here, it translates into cheaper versions of VWs and Audis. Volkswagen is still working out how to balance its various brands.
Brand value: * * *

## SKODA:

another Volkswagen Group brand (see SEAT above). Rear-engined Skodas used to potter around the cobbled streets of Prague. Now Skodas are no laughing matter. Volkswagen engineering makes the smaller ones a sensible buy.
Brand value: * * *

## SMART:

a masterpiece of marketing. Smart (part-designed by a watchmaker) is DaimlerChrysler's urban-chic tiddler, with derivative

names like Passion that could be dated by 2005. Retained values are looking good and the introduction of the Roadster keeps the brand fresh.
Brand value: * * * *

## SUBARU:

low-profile owners quietly rave about these Japanese cars. They ensure Subaru continues to do well in the JD Power survey (an American evaluation of owners' views, loved by winners, discredited by losers). The dependable characteristics of the models are matched by their ability to hold their values.
Brand value: * * *

## SUZUKI:

a motorcycle manufacturer that is still trying to feel as assured in the car business. The range of cars is too large and there are no stars.
Brand value: *

## TOYOTA:

a brand going places, and mostly in the right direction. Yaris was the best new small car from a Japanese manufacturer. Avensis is cheap on the used car market because it is so dull. Applaud Toyota for the Prius (runs at times on battery-power) because it anticipates future legislation. Toyota will keep getting better.
Brand value: * * * *

## TVR:

made-in-Blackpool and strictly for enthusiasts (mainly male) who love the red-blooded performance. Performance is a higher priority than electronic safety aids. Not as suave as Porsche but the brand value is individuality.
Brand value: * * *

## VAUXHALL:

brand value remains uncertain as it desperately tries to shed its worthy-but-dull image with coupes and convertibles. The Astra is a classic used car star. It is far better than its image suggests, so can be a genuine bargain.
Brand value: * * *

## VOLKSWAGEN:

expertly plays on its image as a manufacturer obsessed with quality and good engineering. Polo, Golf and Passat are all strong players in their classes. The Beetle was more exciting as a styling exercise. As a brand, VW will have something to prove in 2004-06.
Brand value: * * *

## VOLVO:

Ford bought it to have a presence in the large car market after dropping the Scorpio. Volvo's brand value was built on safety but rivals have moved ahead with electronic wizardry to avoid use of the crumple zones whenever possible. For Volvo, 2004-06 is critical in terms of brand image.
Brand value: * * *

## Chapter 14

# Set a budget

### HP, PCP, a loan or cash ... decide what's best for you as a way of buying a car

"Put down the biggest deposit you can afford – the faster the repayment, the less it costs you"

'All gain, no pain ... the Lotus Elise from £199 per month.' This was the tantalising headline on a sales leaflet which seemed to put the charismatic little sports car within easy reach of us all.

Alongside the headline was a picture of an attractive young couple in dark glasses, each with a hand resting on an Elise. But in brackets (where reality kicks in) were the words 'plus deposit, fees and final payment – APR 7.5%'. Car makers need to grab your attention with a compelling message. They seek to retain it until your signature is on an order form. But they are also obliged to spell out the whole story, as Lotus did in precise detail. Part of that process means admitting that the finance figures related to a £23,385 Elise 1.8 convertible, while the car in the photograph was the 111S that costs £5,000 more. It is not unusual for car companies to use an upgraded derivative for a picture in a brochure, or to add fancy alloy wheels. Always read the small print, because it will be

explained somewhere. The Lotus leaflet worked because the product was so desirable that many people at least flirted with the idea of ownership. They could find the deposit of £7,950 and also the monthly repayments: one of £294, then 35 of £199. But the unpalatable bit was the requirement to make a final payment of £11,135.01. This took the total amount payable to £26,344.01. Even so, the cost of financing the deal was just under £3,000. Conditions of this deal included purchase from a Lotus franchised dealer, by a private buyer and within a short time frame. The insider method is to decide whether a

**INSIDER GUIDE TO DEALER FINANCE**

These are the top rules when borrowing money to buy a car:

- Dealers get high commission on loans with very low deposits: check that the interest rate is not unfavourably high
- Do not give dealers all your personal details before committing yourself to a loan: they may contact other lenders in the hope of earning a higher commission.
- Put down the biggest deposit you can afford: the faster the repayment, the less it costs you
- Check out terms from different lenders
- Check the APR (annual interest rate)
- Compare loan amount and terms in each case
- Offer something as security on the loan: it is cheaper than when unsecured.
- Ask to see your credit record if a loan is refused
- Contact the lender if you cannot keep up the repayments
- Consider a payment protection scheme
- Get fully comprehensive insurance cover on the car, otherwise you could be liable to pay off the loan if the vehicle is a write-off
- Always read the small print

SOURCE: PARKER'S CAR CHOOSER

purchase method in a sales campaign works best for you, or whether it would be better to consider an alternative way of buying such as via the internet, an importer, or a private sale.

Finance deals can be a pointer to the standing of a manufacturer and its self-confidence. Fiat went into the automotive confessional box in early 2003 by offering 0 per cent finance with no deposit on all its cars. This was as near as it gets to long-term renting, with the chance (in round figures) to run a £12,000 Fiat Stilo Multiwagon (estate) for £500 a month for two years. Of the other nine ways to buy examined earlier, checking out car

supermarkets would have been a good alternative if you wanted a Fiat. If a manufacturer is struggling with sales, some of its sticking stock is likely to be offered at car supermarkets. When manufacturers have to resort to this type of distress selling, the volume of extra sales can reduce the value of the car by the time your payments have finished. If you are tempted by any finance package carefully constructed by a manufacturer, you need to take all the figures into account. With low interest rates, finance deals are an effective way for manufacturers to boost sales. In a short-term offer to pep up late-autumn sales, Vauxhall ran a free loan scheme, commonly referred to as 0 per cent finance. It cut the deposit to 20 per cent from the 40 per cent or more normally demanded by manufacturers. The offer was restricted to five derivatives of the Corsa and Astra. It looked a good deal as long as you really wanted one of the cars, but the model has to be the starting point, not the finance package. High street banks, supermarkets and other direct lenders are working hard to promote loans to private buyers. This is posing serious problems for dealers who gain a commission on the loan and, with profit margins on new cars slimmer than ever, do not want to lose this additional source of revenue.

The advantage in negotiating a loan before beginning your research is the flexibility it gives in exploring the different ways of buying. If you are most comfortable with buying from a franchised dealer, you should still shop around for the finance. If you can pay the deposit on a car that includes the offer of 0 per cent finance to pay off the balance, this could be an attractive proposition. But the obvious still needs stating. Even with low interest rates, hefty monthly repayments still put a strain on your finances.

Ways of financing the purchase of cars are opening up in much the same way as the methods of buying one. Hire purchase is being made to seem old-fashioned because of the growth of personal contract purchase (PCP) and personal contract hire (PCH) but it remains the most popular type of

 ## INSIDER GUIDE TO CAR LOAN SOURCES

Ask your bank about a loan to buy a car and pick up a leaflet from your supermarket. This will provide a starting point for an assessment of terms available. Some companies offering car loans are listed below (there are many others). Use Google or another search engine to go to the website of one you want to explore).

**AA**
www.theaa.com
0800 616 383

**Goldfish**
www.goldfish.com
0800 885 555

**Alliance & Leicester**
www.alliance-leicester.co.uk/cars
08705 555 555

**Lombard Direct**
www.lombarddirect.com
0800 215 000

**Direct Line**
www.directline.com
0845 246 7788

**RAC**
www.rac.co.uk
0808 1000 250

## GRAND CONTENDER

## MERCEDES-BENZ S-CLASS

 **NEW** CAR SAYS...

**FOR** Luxury, dynamics, fine diesel engine
**AGAINST** Expensive at top of range
**SUM UP** Still the best plutobarge

 **USED** (1991-99)
**PARKER'S CHOOSER SAYS...**

**FOR** Pedigree; quality; engineering
**AGAINST** Size; sky-high running costs; 'fat cat' image
**VALUE** Obsolete but retains some prestige; monster depreciation – buy mid-Nineties example for best value

arranges a loan on the outstanding amount and picks up a commission. You repay the amount borrowed plus interest to the finance company over an agreed period. After making a token final payment, you own the car although you must not sell it during the loan period without informing the lender.

PCPs have become popular because monthly repayments are lower than when buying on HP. This is because you do not pay for the car, but for the value it loses over the period of the agreement. The final payment is based on an estimate of what the car will be worth and it is usually possible to get a minimum guaranteed final value (MGFV), though this will be conditional on the condition of the car and its mileage. You can pay it, and the car is yours, or decline to pay and hand the car back. The third way is to trade the car in for a new one and this normally works out as the best option. It means PCPs make most sense if you want to buy a new car every two or three years. It is part of the reason car manufacturers run PCP schemes with branded names. They make money from the finance deal, encourage people to adopt a regular new-car habit and, importantly, attempt to encourage brand loyalty.

Volkswagen's package is typical. It was originally called Solutions but was re-launched as New Solutions. For company car drivers taking the cash instead, there is New Solutions Cash4Car. Some employers are giving their company car drivers the chance to opt out of the scheme, buy a car of their choice and receive an annual cash payment to cover business travel. All

credit agreement. It is simple and there are no penalty clauses if the mileage turns out to be higher than you expected by the end of the agreement. Hire purchase is so called because you agree to hire the car before making a final 'option to purchase' fee at the end of the contract. HP continues to

appeal to many because it can be speedily arranged with a dealer. After deducting the deposit, and taking into account any part exchange, the dealer manufacturers operate these schemes. Check their websites to compare them. For those with a computer, all can be located by keying the manufacturer's name into Google or another internet search engine.

Opt for personal contract hire (also known as personal leasing), and you never own the car, which is handed back at the end of the agreed period. In effect, this is a long-term rental arrangement and it is popular in the US but taking time to become established in the UK. The deposit is low but monthly payments are high. A variation is lease purchase. You negotiate a deposit and the monthly instalments and it then operates rather like an HP agreement. The difference is that at the end, you have to make a final 'balloon' payment. Monthly payments can be kept low if you agree a high final payment: after

paying it, the car is yours. Before a loan is advanced, you will be asked for details of your financial standing including your income, mortgage and credit cards. This information will be passed to a credit reference agency that will use public records to check for debts registered over the past six years and any county court judgements against you. You should ask any finance company that refuses credit to explain why. Under the Data Protection Act, you can search your record at the relevant credit reference agency. The lender is obliged to identify it and you can then correct any errors in your records.

Lex Vehicle Leasing (www.lvl.co.uk) has a comprehensive website guide to leasing schemes for private motorists and company car drivers. It also provides an online calculator for company drivers thinking of opting for

## INSIDER GUIDE TO LOAN ADVICE

**Car Credit Centre**
(independent car loan broker)
www.carcreditcentre.com
0800 904 7982

**Easy Quote**
(web-based comparisons)
www.easy-quote.co.uk

**Fast Track Car Loans**
(loan comparisons)
www.fasttrack-loans.co.uk/car-loans
020 8771 2875

**Finance and Leasing Association**
(UK finance company regulator and trade body)
www.fla.org.uk
020 7836 6511

**Shopper UK**
(loan comparisons and quick links to many lenders)
www.shopperuk.com

'cash for cars'. In some circumstances, people can pay less tax this way.

Since April 2002, company car benefit in kind (BIK) has been based on $CO_2$ exhaust emissions instead of mileage. Employers are not obliged to enter into one of these agreements and the other disadvantage is that high business mileage affects the value of your car. The potential to run a nearly new car or to buy an import is part of the appeal, especially for those bored by anonymous 'repmobiles'. Also, a change of job means you can keep the same car, as long as the new employer runs a cash-for-cars programme.

For everyone, company car user or private car buyer, the vehicle makes a statement about you every day you are at the wheel. This is why the selection of the model must always come before the way it is bought or leased.

## GRAND CONTENDER

## MG TF

 **NEW** CAR SAYS...

**FOR** Old fashioned roadster motoring

**AGAINST** Handling still unresolved

**SUM UP** Back to the old school

 **USED** (MGF – 1991-99) PARKER'S CHOOSER SAYS...

**FOR** Styling; handling; brand heritage

**AGAINST** Dated interior; patchy build quality

**VALUE** Launch of MGTF has brought MGF prices down. MGTF well equipped except for the basic 115. Options expensive

Chapter 15

# An ever-changing industry

## Manufacturers are always under pressure – private buyers always have time on their side

"The car is the object of love/hate relationships for tens of millions of owners"

We have focused so far on the 10 different ways to buy a car, examined how manufacturers and the motor trade encourage you to make a purchase and looked at the power brands and ways of buying. The car is a commodity in the eyes of the global industry that makes it, but it would be remiss to end this book without some words to celebrate the car, the object of love/hate relationships for tens of millions of owners.

The motor industry was born more than a century ago. At the outset there was scepticism over whether powered vehicles would ever replace horse-drawn carriages. Today the majority of people on the planet either have a car, or aspire to own or use one.

The industry and its products are in a constant state of change. The process is somewhat like the Darwinian theory of the evolution of life on Earth which begins: 'On the origin of species by means of natural selection, or the preservation of favoured races in the struggle for life...'. He could have been writing about the motor industry.

As a buyer, you are tapping into a vast industry, populated by staff and companies driven by powerful forces that can result in heady success or crushing failure. A few of the people and the cars they design and build become icons. Henry Ford, the creator of assembly line manufacturing, was one, and Britain's Mini, born in 1959, another. Hundreds of models come and go, liked or even loved by some but ignored by many because, in the UK at least, the choice is so varied. In the early years, car makers sprang up all over Europe. Enthusiasts produced hand-built cars for wealthy pioneers who brought terror to villages where people and animals previously wandered, disturbed only by the occasional horse-drawn cart or carriage.

Now cars from Europe, North America, South America, Asia and the rest of the world jostle for road space in every developed country. A few tiny producers, such as Morgan and Ferrari, maintain the traditions of the early entrepreneurs but more than 99 per cent of vehicles come from a global machine building millions of cars a year. They all have to go somewhere, and many lack individuality.

That is why you are in control. Confused by the commercial clamour, the buyer can easily be pushed into bad judgements. 'There has never been a better time', is the call. Manufacturers have been saying it for decades. But private buyers always have time on their side. In Europe, if sales in one country are booming, those in another will be struggling, forcing manufacturers to make generous offers to tempt buyers. Manufacturers are always under pressure, always eager for sales. With apologies to Kitchener and his World War I plea: 'Your car manufacturer needs YOU'. Whereas, of course, you can choose anything from a new MINI to a used MPV.

In 2002, the UK achieved record sales of new cars but manufacturers found it hard to make a profit because

## MINI

**NEW** CAR SAYS...
**FOR** Great to drive, great to own
**AGAINST** Cramped, poor early build quality
**SUM UP** Still in fashion

**USED** (1991-99)
PARKER'S CHOOSER SAYS...
**FOR** Slick handling; cool image
**AGAINST** Poor rear space
**VALUE** Competitively priced with generous equipment. Vast array of options allows personalisation

of the investment in winning customers. Markets are force-fed, like geese producing pâté de foie gras. The producers push stock vigorously because without stimulation demand is not strong enough. New car-making countries emerge with lower costs. In 2002, China overtook South Korea in the global car-making league and assembly lines become ever more efficient. It is a relentless process that makes cars cheaper though, for purists, less interesting.

Charles Darwin explained why dodos had their day and then became extinct. In the process of the random selection of species on Earth, many designs are tried but only the strongest survive. So it has been with car manufacturers in the pursuit of sales and market share. Austin, Morris, Triumph, Wolseley and others have been assimilated into Rover. That new company was temporarily owned, in a moment of uncharacteristic bad judgement, by BMW, then sold in a desperate struggle to survive as a

reborn MG Rover. Now MG has an arrangement with a Chinese company to share development costs for a successor to the Metro, which evolved into the Rover 100 and then became extinct. Manufacturers are continuing to consolidate into a few powerful groups. One important incentive is to save money by sharing components among several brands, as Volkswagen Group does with VW, Audi, Skoda and SEAT. It also owns Bentley and Bugatti. These groups want you to trade up to a more exclusive badge as a way of growing profits. However, Volkswagen found to its cost that some consumers take the view that a Skoda is better value than an Audi. So the group has to make new Audis more refined, more desirable... and so it continues. The challenge for the buyer is to balance the value of the car and its badge. This is where the psychology of car buying kicks in. Some people want a car with a glamorous image, while others prefer it to be anonymous. We view cars from different perspectives: Skoda is still seen as a joke by some, others realise it has become a symbol of value, a VW with a new skin that represents a smart buy. When Russian Ladas were sold in the UK, it was difficult to believe their owners could not afford anything better. Manufacturers know that selling on price alone is a perilous path (Proton is an example) and try to improve the image through costly advertising. This has to be achieved in step with new models otherwise potential customers become convinced they are being hoodwinked. Ford Motor Company bought Jaguar, Land Rover and Volvo to re-invent itself, with brands that now outshine Henry's

## GRAND CONTENDER

### VAUXHALL CORSA

### 👎 NEW CAR SAYS...
**FOR** Durable, cute
**AGAINST** Stodgy, outclassed
**SUM UP** Fabia, Fiesta and Micra are all better

### 👍 USED (2000 ON)
**PARKER'S CHOOSER SAYS...**
**FOR** Spacious interior; good looks; refined engines
**AGAINST** Poor quality trim; tight rear cabin space
**VALUE** Well equipped; used prices are already competitive; appears well built, some interior trim a bit skimpy

## MITSUBISHI SPACE WAGON

### NEW CAR SAYS...
**FOR** Big, sensible
**AGAINST** Boring
**SUM UP** Can't get near Espace

### USED (1998 ON)
### PARKER'S CHOOSER SAYS...
**FOR** Practical; compact; easy to drive
**AGAINST** Rather bumpy ride; looking their age
**VALUE** Seven-seater all-rounder; can be overpriced

beloved 'blue oval'. The group stopped assembling Ford cars in the UK but has three Jaguar plants – another step in the evolution of car production. Car manufacturers group together to share the high cost of the design, development and production of a new model. DaimlerChrysler is a German-dominated combination of Mercedes-Benz and Smart and America's Chrysler and Jeep. Mercedes is acknowledged as the world's strongest car brand but that perception has been stretched by the A-Class. So the deal was done to supply thousands to the Easy group's venture into car rental.

No manufacturer, not even mighty Mercedes, is immune to the industry's market forces.

People are unnerved by a change in a car manufacturer's strategy because they want to know whether the future value of the car they plan to buy will be affected. And the UK's Mercedes dealers were also unnerved when the manufacturer gave them all a year's notice, later lengthened to two years. Mercedes wants to control (mainly through dealerships it owns and operates) sales in London and other major conurbations. The company is so confident of the desirability of its brand that it is planning a new centre on part of the former Brooklands motor racing circuit in Surrey. This could become a Mecca for Mercedes owners and admirers, a place for people to buy, or where their desire to buy is strengthened. Increasing sales to achieve volumes needed for global price competitiveness puts pressure on a car brand, however good. Mercedes used to count BMW, Audi and Jaguar as its only rivals in Britain and managed to command high enough showroom prices to produce comfortable profits for itself and its dealers. The turning point came with the A-Class model. Dealers could no longer ask customers to form a queue. The A-Class is a volume model with a clever design and a relatively high price.

Meanwhile, volume manufacturers such as Vauxhall/Opel, Renault, Honda and others began to consider moving more into the so-called executive and luxury sectors, a reversal of the decision by Mercedes and its immediate competitors to expand by building cheaper cars. The lines began to be blurred in the early 1990s, one of the reasons prompting Mercedes to build a visitor centre that would be a monument to its achievements in quality engineering, and consolidate an image put at risk by increasing competition. This competition has come from Jaguar (much improved products after a decade of investment by Ford), Lexus (premium brand kept at arm's length from Toyota, its creator), Porsche (now expanding out of pure sports cars into the sports utility market) and others.

Cars like Porsches, BMW coupes, Audi sports saloons and Jaguar cabriolets are often driven by people wanting to celebrate maybe a decade of hard work building up their own business. They will probably not own the car but enter into a contract hire/leasing agreement. People entitled to a company car as part of their job or employment package have demanded a bigger say in the selection of their car as the choice has grown. Apart from directors and senior managers, they would once have been asked to choose from a small selection. But now they have become 'user choosers' and the list of cars available to key staff members can be one of the reasons they stay with a firm or move on.

Manufacturers pay a great deal of attention to the equipment on cars offered in leasing packages. Companies like Alfa Romeo (offering the spirit of Italy, land of speed and warmth) try to entice business drivers away from the German manufacturers with their reputation for long-term reliability and new electronic driving and safety aids. Meanwhile, Ford and Nissan create

sporty derivatives, and Mercedes pitches its C-class against them for business sales that are the bedrock of the industry in Britain. The best profit on each company car comes from so-called user choosers but the volume manufacturers must also find bulk sales. When deals of 1,000 to 20,000 or more cars are announced, the value is quoted 'at showroom prices'. A company with hundreds or thousands of staff needing cars expects to pay a fraction of the listed showroom price – perhaps £10,000 or less for a car with a recommended retail price of £15,000. If you pay the full price, you

## GRAND CONTENDER

### RENAULT MEGANE

**NEW CAR SAYS...**
**FOR** Stylish, fun, different
**AGAINST** Bland chassis
**SUM UP** Deserved its win

**USED PARKER'S CHOOSER SAYS...**
**FOR** Outstanding safety
**AGAINST** Cramped cabin
**VALUE** All models generously equipped – aircon, electric windows and CD standard on most.

are subsidising the business buyers and that means you are honour bound to track down a good deal. Over the past five years, prices of new cars in Britain have been forced down. In August 2000, the Department of Trade and Industry announced measures to increase the competitiveness of the supply and sale of cars. This followed an inquiry by the Competition Commission that ruled UK new car buyers were, on average, paying about 10 per cent (or £1,100) too much. The director general at the Office of Fair Trading estimated that private car buyers could be paying in total around £1bn a year too much. Consumers have helped to push prices down by negotiating harder and exploring new ways of buying. Changes in European law that allow more freedom for car retailers to operate competitively are helping people to find the right car at the right price. To help you make a decision, this book concludes with a keen-eyed evaluation of new cars from *Car* magazine and a pragmatic evaluation of used cars... your quest is the right car for you, bought at the right price.

## INSIDER GUIDE FOR WOMEN BUYERS

Women car drivers complain that the motor trade continues to be sexist – it is something the industry needs to change. A female psychologist with experience of car buying dissects the failings of male showroom staff and explains how women should respond.

*'Women with far more responsible jobs than selling cars feel they are not taken seriously. Most men are more interested in cars than most women, but that is no reason for salesmen to sneer if we lack confidence when asking questions or confess we can't change a wheel.*
*'Remain calm and polite, ask to speak to the manager and quietly explain how you were made to feel.*
*'Intelligent middle-aged women are irritated by the condescending manner of young salesmen who give the impression they are looking over our shoulders for a man who will deal with things.*
*'I have been in car showrooms accompanied by a man and the attitude of staff is entirely different. But I did eventually find a dealership where staff answered my questions directly and put air in my tyres because I'm not confident of doing it properly.. It's the dealership where I now buy cars and have them serviced.'*

## Chapter 16

# Car:

The good, the bad, the ugly

People planning to buy a new car get the chance to try maybe two or three models before making a decision. That's why they rely heavily on magazines that review the vast range available in the UK and assess their good and bad points.

Car magazine has published a survey called 'The good, the bad, the ugly' for many years. It is compiled by the magazine's team of road testers who combine extensive experience with a waspish sense of humour.

Their comments are honest, direct and to the point, which is why manufacturers of 'the bad and ugly' frequently find their toes curling in discomfort.

The appraisals listed on this and the following pages were published in the spring of 2003. Many remain valid but, for the current opinions of the Car team, you need to see the latest issue.

### ALFA ROMEO
**147**
FOR Stylish, fun to drive
AGAINST Not a Golf
SUM UP Italian without the tears

**156**
FOR Gorgeous
AGAINST Italian build quality
SUM UP Cooler than a 3-series

**166**
FOR Rare, revamp is imminent
AGAINST Not extinct
SUM UP Insipid plutobarge reinforces all Italian stereotypes

**GTV/Spider**
FOR Slinky styling, V6 engine
AGAINST Acute depreciation
SUM UP You still would

### ASTON MARTIN
**DB7**
FOR Best-looking Aston ever?
AGAINST Based on Jag XJ-S
SUM UP Makes Vanquish look expensive

**Vanquish**
FOR James Bond drives one
AGAINST He used to have a Z3
SUM UP Yes. Please

## AUDI

### A2
FOR Light, clever
AGAINST Witheringly expensive
SUM UP Not quite the future

### A3
FOR Easy resale assured
AGAINST Stodgy drive, poor kit
SUM UP Big-arsed Golf in a frock

### A4
FOR Build quality
AGAINST Bouncy suspension
SUM UP More exclusive than a 3-series

### A6/S6
FOR Solid
AGAINST Old
SUM UP Consider second-hand only

### A8
FOR Clever tech, alloy build
AGAINST Big Audis never sell
SUM UP Deserves to succeed

### Allroad
FOR Good off-road
AGAINST Otherwise pointless
SUM UP Gymkhana car park

### TT
FOR Wine bar chic
AGAINST Default choice
SUM UP Golf in lingerie

## BENTLEY

### Arnage
FOR As British as the Ark Royal
AGAINST Bigger
SUM UP Still rules da 'hood

### Azure/Continental
FOR One of a kind
AGAINST How much?
SUM UP Ultimate conspicuous consumption

## BMW

### 3-Series
FOR Best car in segment
AGAINST Every man and his dog has one
SUM UP Woof woof woof

### 5-Series
FOR Still great
AGAINST Dies soon
SUM UP Hard to say no

### 7-Series
FOR Clever
AGAINST Too clever by half
SUM UP Cyborg killer limo, feels neither pity nor remorse

### Z4
FOR Massively better than Z3
AGAINST Not quite a Boxster
SUM UP You wouldn't regret your decision if you bought one

### X5
FOR Big, brutish, gets respect, drives well
AGAINST Horribly offensive
SUM UP Penis envy

## BRISTOL

### Blenheim
FOR British
AGAINST Pricey, antiquated
SUM UP Eccentric

## CADILLAC

### CTS
FOR Crisp styling
AGAINST Optimised for American roads
SUM UP We've yet to drive it....

## CATERHAM

### Seven
FOR Peerless driving experience
AGAINST In dog years it's 315
SUM UP Perfect... as a second car

## CHRYSLER

### Neon
FOR Nothing
AGAINST Everything
SUM UP Don't even go there

### PT Cruiser
FOR It's different
AGAINST It's different
SUM UP The joke has long since faded

### Voyager
FOR Big
AGAINST The Espace is better
SUM UP Putting the 'van' in minivan

## CITROEN

### Saxo
FOR Cheap, cheerful
AGAINST Tissue box construction
SUM UP Better than walking

### C3
FOR Looks great
AGAINST Drives badly
SUM UP An opportunity missed

### Xsara
FOR Value FOR money
AGAINST Froggy styling, ancient
underpinnings
SUM UP Still priced to sell

### C5
FOR Big, diesels, equipment
AGAINST Ugly, auction-fodder depreciation
SUM UP Perfect minicab

### Berlingo
FOR Seriously useful
AGAINST Because it's a van
SUM UP A VFM bargain

### Picasso
FOR Big, different, good value
AGAINST Surrealist nuance makes it more
Dali-esque
SUM UP Pickle it in formaldehyde

### C8
FOR Enormous and very well equipped
AGAINST It's still a van
SUM UP Betters Peugeot sister

## DAEWOO
### Matiz
FOR Cheap, fun, fizzy 800cc engine
AGAINST 'I don't know anything about cars'
image
SUM UP So cheap it makes sense

### Daewoo Tacuma
FOR Useful MPV type thing
AGAINST Utterly horrible styling
SUM UP Daewoo's least weak link

### Daewoo Kalos
FOR Not bad-looking
AGAINST For a Daewoo
SUM UP Still a Daewoo

## DAIHATSU
### Cuore
FOR Cheapest Japanese-built car in the UK
AGAINST Flimsy, slow, dull
SUM UP Automotive porridge

### Sirion
FOR Amusing to drive, fast Rally 2
AGAINST Looks like a dead frog
SUM UP Odd but fun

### YRV
FOR Funky, spacious, 4wd option
AGAINST Silly name (Young Recreational
Vehicle), silly looks
SUM UP Worth considering

### Terios
FOR Looks butch
AGAINST Isn't
SUM UP Utterly pointless miniaturised
pretend SUV

### Fourtrak
FOR Farmers love them
AGAINST Farmers love them
SUM UP Farmers love them

## FERRARI
### 360
FOR Looks, handling, performance, sound
AGAINST 911 Turbo does more
SUM UP Pretty near perfect

### 456
FOR Utterly beautiful
AGAINST Fiat Tipo switchgear
SUM UP Old but gorgeous

### 575M
FOR Awesomely competent grand tourer
AGAINST Softer-edged than 550
SUM UP Still the daddy

## FIAT
### Seicento
FOR Cheap
AGAINST Nasty
SUM UP Seriously outclassed

### Punto
FOR Durable, spacious
AGAINST Trails Fabia, Fiesta, Jazz
SUM UP Only makes sense cheap

### Stilo
FOR Loaded with gadgets
AGAINST They should have focused on the
car underneath
SUM UP Fiat's future looks shaky

## Stilo Multi Wagon
FOR Spacious load area
AGAINST Only five seats
SUM UP Just an estate with a good view

## Marea
FOR Imminent replacement
AGAINST Everything else
SUM UP Was off the pace five years ago

## Barchetta
FOR Looks lovely, goes well
AGAINST Left-hand drive
SUM UP Seems neglected, which is a shame

## Doblo
FOR It's very big
AGAINST It's very, very ugly
SUM UP Berlingo and Kangoo rule this segment

## Multipla
FOR Daring design, good to drive
AGAINST Popular prejudice
SUM UP People don't know what they're missing

## Ulysse
FOR Couriers love them
AGAINST Because they're vans
SUM UP Just can't get excited

# FORD
## Ka
FOR Cute, tough, great to drive
AGAINST Cramped
SUM UP The ideal first car

## Fiesta
FOR Space, dynamic prowess
AGAINST Lacks surprise or delight
SUM UP Brilliant to drive, otherwise feels cheap

## Fusion
FOR It's slightly taller than a Fiesta
AGAINST That's it
SUM UP Bone idle lazy

## Focus
FOR Looks, handling, engines
AGAINST Stingy kit
SUM UP Still the one to beat

## Mondeo
FOR The rep's favourite
AGAINST Cheap construction
SUM UP A million user-choosers can't be wrong

## Galaxy
FOR VW construction
AGAINST Ford badge
SUM UP Getting old quickly

# HONDA
## Jazz
FOR Spacious, clever, solid
AGAINST Pricey
SUM UP It's boss supermini

## Civic
FOR Daring looks, clever design
AGAINST Boring, except Type-R
SUM UP Consummate all-rounder

## Insight
FOR Planet-saving hybrid
AGAINST Only two seats, pious image
SUM UP Join Greenpeace

## Accord
FOR It's new
AGAINST It's still so dull
SUM UP Honda, you can do better than this

## Legend
FOR Big luxo-barge
AGAINST You'd lose it in a car park
SUM UP Too boring to live with

## S2000
FOR Best four-pot engine in the world
AGAINST Snappy chassis
SUM UP Needs respect

## NSX
FOR Sublime dynamics, wonderful engine
AGAINST The cabin is stuck in 1989
SUM UP Seriously consider one

## Stream
FOR An MPV that's great to drive
AGAINST But desperately boring to look at
SUM UP The future

## CR-V
FOR Painlessly competent soft-roader
AGAINST Lacks presence
SUM UP Yawn

## HR-V
FOR Down with the kids
AGAINST Minority taste
SUM UP Hormone replacement vehicle

## HYUNDAI

### Getz
FOR Class competitive
AGAINST Boring
SUM UP A warranty this good makes it a serious contender

### Accent
FOR Cheap
AGAINST Unpleasant to drive, silly to look at
SUM UP Must try harder

### Elantra
FOR Drives well, lots of kit
AGAINST Looks silly, depreciates brutally
SUM UP Great secondhand buy

### Sonata
FOR Big, wafty, loadsa kit
AGAINST Chrome detailing
SUM UP It's a Korean pretend Cadillac

### XG30
FOR As Sonata
AGAINST Only bigger
SUM UP Wonderfully pointless

### Coupe
FOR Nice to drive, cheap, great V6 engine
AGAINST Crappy cabin
SUM UP Greatest Korean car. Ever

### Matrix
FOR Is it an MPV?
AGAINST Or a mutated hatchback?
SUM UP Priced within special-offer Picasso territory

### Trajet
FOR Espace size FOR Megane dosh
AGAINST Kia Sedona is cheaper
SUM UP Sounds too like a Bee Gees song title

### Santa Fe
FOR Porsche-designed powertrain
AGAINST Genetically modified look
SUM UP Restyled out of contention

## ISUZU

### Trooper
FOR It's called Bighorn in Japan
AGAINST Surprisingly average off-roader
SUM UP Leave it to the farmers

## JAGUAR

### X-type
FOR Badge
AGAINST Mondeo DNA shows
SUM UP Can't get close to segment leaders

### S-type
FOR Relaxed, old fashioned dynamics
AGAINST Retro styling
SUM UP An acquired taste

### XJ8
FOR Hi-tech alloy construction
AGAINST Looks identical to its steel predecessor
SUM UP A truly modern classic

### XK8
FOR Gorgeous looks, outstanding performance
AGAINST 911 money
SUM UP Still a compelling option

## JEEP

### Cherokee
FOR Tough, rugged, king of the school run
AGAINST Thirsty, old fashioned
SUM UP Get soft-roader instead

### Grand Cherokee
FOR Big, solid, well equipped
AGAINST Slightly overspecced FOR shopping in Twickenham
SUM UP Ironic not iconic

### Wrangler
FOR Queer as folk
AGAINST Renegade
SUM UP Its moment passed in 1945

## KIA

### Rio
FOR She dances in the sand
AGAINST Like a river twisting through a dusty land
SUM UP And when she shines...

### Shuma
FOR Warranty
AGAINST Dynamic superiority of beige Maestros they replace
SUM UP Horrible

### Mentor
FOR Cheap
AGAINST Nasty
SUM UP Hatchback Shuma, equally horrible

**Magentis**
FOR Big, wafty, well constructed
AGAINST Zero image, massive depreciation
SUM UP Parallel universe Cadillac

**Carens**
FOR Mini MPV so loads of space
AGAINST Boring, invisible, ugly
SUM UP Makes the Citroen Berlingo look attractive

**Sedona**
FOR Big, huge, ginormous
AGAINST Like steering an ocean liner
SUM UP Unbeatable value

**Sportage**
FOR It's a sort of proto-soft-roader
AGAINST Useless off-road and on
SUM UP Justifiably rare

## LAMBORGHINI
**Murcielago**
FOR The last true supercar
AGAINST Faint whiff of chest wig
SUM UP Still the ultimate bedroom wall accessory

## LAND ROVER
**Freelander**
FOR Painless on-road
AGAINST Pointless off-road
SUM UP Elastic brand engineering

**Discovery**
FOR Better than it used to be
AGAINST Still not great
SUM UP Fashion is a cruel mistress

**Range Rover**
FOR It's a monster off-roader, it's a luxury car
AGAINST Drinks oil fields whole
SUM UP Great, if you can afford it

**Defender**
FOR Still unrivalled in the bog
AGAINST Panel gaps visible from space
SUM UP A true British icon

## LEXUS
**IS**
FOR Like a 3-series only Japanese
AGAINST Lacks personality
SUM UP Highly attractive package

**GS**
FOR Very reliable
AGAINST Old, plasticky, no match FOR BMW or Merc
SUM UP FOR limo companies only

**LS**
FOR Probably the best-equipped car in the world
AGAINST Breeze block styling
SUM UP Viable S-class alternative

**RX**
FOR Nice to drive on the road but no X5
AGAINST Replaced very soon
SUM UP Wait FOR RX330

**SC**
FOR Clever folding hard-top
AGAINST Is so last season
SUM UP Like a 206 CC, only £40k more expensive

## LOTUS
**Elise**
FOR An incredible driving experience
AGAINST Camp retro styling
SUM UP Rediscover driving joy

## MARCOS
**Marcasite**
FOR Individual alternative to mainstream roadsters
AGAINST Pricey FOR what you get
SUM UP Only FOR freethinkers

## MASERATI
**Coupe**
FOR Italian style, convincing performance
AGAINST Awful F1-style gearshift
SUM UP As a manual it's lovely

**Spyder**
FOR Like the Coupe but with more fresh air
AGAINST Slightly wobbly structure
SUM UP Brave to compete with XK

## MAZDA
**2**
FOR Cabin space and styling
AGAINST Ride isn't great, adverts
SUM UP Based on the Fiesta but feels very different, good value

**323**
FOR Painless to own
AGAINST Completely featureless in every respect
SUM UP Yawn, wait FOR the 3...

## 6
FOR Great chassis, Mondeo-beating dynamics
AGAINST Noisy engines, poor CO2
SUM UP A future fleet favourite

## Premacy
FOR Spacious little MPV
AGAINST It's no Multipla
SUM UP Too dull FOR serious consideration

## MPV
FOR Does exactly what it says on the tin
AGAINST And nothing else
SUM UP Unimaginative

## MX-5
FOR Handling, performance, durability
AGAINST Basic and expensive
SUM UP Still supreme fun

## Tribute
FOR Tribute to what, exactly?
AGAINST Doesn't seem to exist
SUM UP Have you ever seen one?

## MCC
### SMART
FOR Parking
AGAINST Understeer
SUM UP Not quite the future of personal transportation

## MERCEDES
### A-class
FOR Durable, cute, right badge
AGAINST Stodgy to drive
SUM UP One of Merc's more imaginative moments

### C-class
FOR Big FOR its segment, smooth to drive
AGAINST Chronically overpriced
SUM UP 3-series is superior

### E-Class
FOR Big, nice to drive, well equipped
AGAINST Pricey, plasticky cabin
SUM UP Best 5-series alternative

### S-class
FOR Luxury, dynamics, fine diesel engine
AGAINST Expensive at top of range
SUM UP Still the best plutobarge

## CLK Coupe
FOR Looks great, goes well
AGAINST Whiney supercharged engines
SUM UP Stunner

## CLK Cabriolet
FOR Cast iron residuals
AGAINST Replaced soon, too expensive
SUM UP Old model rumbles on

## CL
FOR S-class based coupe
AGAINST Poor residuals
SUM UP If only all Mercs looked this elegant

## SL
FOR An icon redefined, superb
AGAINST Two-year waiting list FOR 55 AMG
SUM UP How the other half live

## SLK
FOR Trick roof, impressive value
AGAINST Soft-edged
SUM UP All most people will ever need

## V-Class
FOR Hire companies love them
AGAINST Because they're Sprinter vans
SUM UP Merc should be ashamed

## M-Class
FOR Upmarket 4x4
AGAINST Outclassed by X5
SUM UP You'd have to really want the badge

## MG ROVER
### 25
FOR Residual Honda reliability
AGAINST Ancient, creaky, overpriced
SUM UP Totally outclassed

### ZR
FOR Great handling
AGAINST Cheesy looks
SUM UP Worth a punt

### 45
FOR It's British
AGAINST It's awful
SUM UP Britain's second worst car

### ZS
FOR Great handling, fun performance
AGAINST It's a polished turd
SUM UP A secondhand bargain

## 75
FOR Smooth, relaxing, well built
AGAINST Slow, excessively retro
SUM UP An acquired taste

## ZT
FOR Fun to drive, good to look at
AGAINST Thirsty V6, abrasive ride
SUM UP MGR's most convincing product to date

## TF
FOR Old-fashioned roadster motoring
AGAINST Handling still unresolved
SUM UP Back to the old school

## MINI
FOR Great to drive, great to own
AGAINST Cramped, poor early build quality
SUM UP Still in fashion

## MITSUBISHI
### Colt
FOR Completely unmemorable
AGAINST Sorry, what?
SUM UP Half past three

### Carisma
FOR Recyclable
AGAINST Completely awful
SUM UP Avoid at all costs

### Lancer Evo VIIi
FOR Mentally fast, increased civility
AGAINST Guaranteed to lose your licence
SUM UP The PlayStation supercar

### Galant
FOR Well built, wafty
AGAINST Vertical depreciation
SUM UP Secondhand bargain

### Space Star
FOR Big space, supermini dimensions
AGAINST Dull
SUM UP But worthy

### Space wagon
FOR Big, sensible
AGAINST Boring
SUM UP Can't get near Espace

### Shogun Pinin
FOR Compact, cute
AGAINST Crude to drive, nasty on road
SUM UP Hard to raise enthusiasm

## Shogun Sport
FOR Good at towing
AGAINST Loud, rough, based on a pick-up
SUM UP Doesn't belong here

## Shogun
FOR Big, brutish, good in the mud
AGAINST Feels very old fashioned
SUM UP How SUVs used to be

## MORGAN
### 4/4 and Plus 8
FOR As English as Terry Thomas eating fish and chips
AGAINST '30s dynamics
SUM UP Only FOR the dedicated

### Aero 8
FOR Great engine and fun to drive
AGAINST It's boss-eyed
SUM UP An unlikely hero

## NISSAN
### Micra
FOR New, funky, cool
AGAINST Cramped in the back
SUM UP This season's supermini

### Almera
FOR Well built
AGAINST Bland, drab, cheap-feeling
SUM UP Leagues below the Focus

### Primera
FOR Funky styling, excellent kit
AGAINST Indifferent to drive
SUM UP Mid-ranking repbox

### Almera Tino
FOR Tough
AGAINST Uninspired and uninspiring
SUM UP Too boring to consider

### X-trail
FOR Line-of-least-resistance soft-roader
AGAINST It's utterly dull
SUM UP Could do worse

### Terrano
FOR Good in the mud
AGAINST Awful everywhere else
SUM UP Britain's worst car

### Patrol
FOR UN peacekeepers love 'em
AGAINST Too wide FOR British width restrictors
SUM UP Right car, wrong country

## PERODUA
**Kelisa**
FOR Durable
AGAINST Utterly insipid
SUM UP 0/10

**Kenari**
FOR (silence)
AGAINST Generally all-round awful
SUM UP Not even worth its modest asking price

## PEUGEOT
**106**
FOR Fun, cheap, popular with students
AGAINST Ancient, crashes badly
SUM UP Its moment has passed

**206**
FOR Funky, fun to drive and in fashion
AGAINST Plasticky cabins
SUM UP Deservedly popular

**206 SW**
FOR Just like any other 206
AGAINST Hardly bigger
SUM UP Rivals are bigger

**307**
FOR European Car of the Year
AGAINST Last year
SUM UP Decent quality and stylish too

**307 SW**
FOR Full-length glass sunroof
AGAINST Otherwise 307 estate
SUM UP Not a viable MPV

**406**
FOR Great to drive, well equipped
AGAINST Ancient, vicious depreciation
SUM UP Consider secondhand

**406 Coupe**
FOR Beautiful, great to drive
AGAINST Expensive
SUM UP Still a stunner after all these years

**607**
FOR Big
AGAINST French
SUM UP When will they learn?

**807**
FOR Takes the whole family
AGAINST They won't want to be seen in it
SUM UP It's a bus

## PORSCHE
**Boxster**
FOR Stunning to drive, great to own, gorgeous
AGAINST Nothing serious
SUM UP Work of genius

**911**
FOR Still a peerless experience
AGAINST Costly to run
SUM UP If you can then you must

**Porsche Cayenne**
FOR Porsche badge
AGAINST Attached to a tank
SUM UP Completely without reason

## PROTON
**Satria**
FOR Based on Mitsubishi Colt
AGAINST Zzzzzz
SUM UP Popular in Malaysia

**Wira**
FOR Amusing name
AGAINST Unamusing car
SUM UP Ghastly

**Impian**
FOR Slightly better than other Protons
AGAINST Still awful
SUM UP Buy a Maestro

## RENAULT
**Clio**
FOR Well priced, fun
AGAINST Less-than-robust cabin
SUM UP Still makes sense

**Megane**
FOR Stylish, fun, different
AGAINST Bland chassis
SUM UP Deserved its win

**Laguna**
FOR Loves the fast lane
AGAINST Doesn't like corners
SUM UP It's a repbox

**Vel satis**
FOR Big, well-constructed cabin
AGAINST Styling, ride, handling
SUM UP French ministerial limo

**Avantime**
FOR It's different
AGAINST Very different
SUM UP Too different

**Kangoo**
FOR Unpretentious utilo-van
AGAINST Pricey here compared to France
SUM UP Cheap and useful

**Megane Scenic**
FOR Still one of the most interesting baby MPVs
AGAINST Increasingly outclassed
SUM UP Wait FOR the new one

**Espace**
FOR The Rolls-Royce of MPVs
AGAINST Less useful than it used to be
SUM UP Still on pole position

## ROLLS-ROYCE

**Phantom**
FOR Massive presence
AGAINST Massive presence
SUM UP Out of my way, little man

## SAAB

**9-3**
FOR Brawn star torque
AGAINST Flaccid cabin
SUM UP Swedish softcore

**9-5**
FOR Fun, solid, safe
AGAINST Feeling very old, sheds value
SUM UP One FOR the brave

## SEAT

**Arosa**
FOR Sounds like a sex toy
AGAINST Vibrates like a sex toy
SUM UP Avoid the 1.0-litre

**Ibiza**
FOR Fabia platform
AGAINST Just not as good
SUM UP Almost, but not quite

**Leon**
FOR Cheapest Golf clone
AGAINST Scratchy naff cabin
SUM UP Sensible bargain

**Toledo**
FOR As good as the Leon
AGAINST It's got a boot
SUM UP Unlikely to ever catch on

**Alhambra**
FOR Sharan FOR a saving
AGAINST Old and outclassed
SUM UP Yes at the right price

## SKODA

**Fabia**
FOR A real quality item
AGAINST Pricey at the top of range
SUM UP The biggest-feeling supermini

**Octavia**
FOR It's another of those Golf clones
AGAINST Overpriced next to Leon
SUM UP Little point, VRS aside

**Superb**
FOR Passat underpinnings
AGAINST No apparent purpose
SUM UP Perfect limo, but FOR badge

## SUBARU

**Impreza**
FOR Slightly less ugly than before
AGAINST Still no looker
SUM UP Perfect on British B roads

**Legacy**
FOR Like an Impreza but bigger, less ugly
AGAINST Seriously thirsty
SUM UP Mostly FOR farmers

**Forester**
FOR Owns the zeitgeist
AGAINST Rolly handling and thirsty
SUM UP Far more sensible than an SUV

## SUZUKI

**Swift**
FOR Very little
AGAINST Everything else
SUM UP Outclassed by every rival

**Liana**
FOR Big cabin
AGAINST Cheapo construction
SUM UP Buy a Space Star instead

**Ignis**
FOR Cutesy looks
AGAINST Insipid dynamics
SUM UP Nul points

**Wagon R**
FOR Useful
AGAINST Silly
SUM UP Not if you've got any dignity

**Jimny**
FOR The list is empty
AGAINST Horrible to drive, own, look at
SUM UP Will always finish last

### Grand Vitara
FOR Used to be in fashion
AGAINST Isn't any more
SUM UP Too expensive and crude next to soft-roaders

## TOYOTA

### Yaris
FOR Charismatic, fun to drive
AGAINST Crashy ride, tiny cabin
SUM UP Loses out to the newer, bigger superminis

### Yaris Verso
FOR Increased practicality
AGAINST Rather less attractive
SUM UP Adds space to Yaris virtues

### Corolla
FOR Completely inoffensive
AGAINST Completely unexciting
SUM UP Transport

### Corolla Verso
FOR Also an MPV
AGAINST Only seats five
SUM UP What's the point?

### Prius
FOR It's totally saving the world, dude
AGAINST Slow, ugly, nasty drive
SUM UP We'd go diesel every time

### Avensis
FOR Unpretentious, quite good
AGAINST Huge fleet sales, awful residuals
SUM UP Three-year-old bargain

### Camry
FOR Americans love it
AGAINST Their roads are straight
SUM UP Totally unsuited to Europe

### Avensis Verso
FOR It's a people-carrying Avensis
AGAINST That's it
SUM UP As exciting as cribbage

### Previa
FOR Enormous, funky rear doors
AGAINST Slabby looks
SUM UP Strong diesels but Voyager and Espace are better

### MR2
FOR Pin-sharp handling
AGAINST Zero luggage space
SUM UP Superb little package

### Celica
FOR A 21st century Japanese Capri
AGAINST Lacks performance
SUM UP One FOR the poseurs

### Rav 4
FOR The most car-like soft-roader
AGAINST Looks silly, can't go off-road
SUM UP Still pointless

### Land Cruiser
FOR New, enormous, towering
AGAINST Overpriced
SUM UP Too big FOR Britain

### Land Cruiser Amazon
FOR Big, big, big
AGAINST Way too big
SUM UP Depends how you regard big

## TVR

### Tamora
FOR The best TVR yet
AGAINST That's not saying much
SUM UP Blood-spitting bulldog

### Tuscan
FOR Massive performance
AGAINST Build quality, brakes
SUM UP Expensively acquired taste

## VAUXHALL

### Agila
FOR Tall, spacious
AGAINST Looks very stupid
SUM UP So easy to understand lack of sales success

### Corsa
FOR Durable, cute
AGAINST Stodgy, outclassed
SUM UP Fabia, Fiesta and Micra are all better

### Astra
FOR Tough as old boots
AGAINST Similar styling
SUM UP Completely inoffensive

### Vectra
FOR Better built than Mondeo
AGAINST Worse to drive
SUM UP Better than before

### Omega
FOR You'll look like a copper
AGAINST Suicidal depreciation
SUM UP The end of an era FOR Vauxhall

## Zafira
FOR Seven seats
AGAINST Stodgy to drive, usually underpowered
SUM UP Deservedly popular

## VX220
FOR It's a rebodied Lotus Elise
AGAINST But with a Griffin badge
SUM UP In turbo guise no car is quicker FOR the money

## Frontera
FOR Jurassic leftover
AGAINST Fossilised
SUM UP Completely out of its depth

## VOLKSWAGEN
### Lupo
FOR Small, cute
AGAINST Tinny, crashy
SUM UP It's no Ka

### Polo
FOR Strong, quality vibes
AGAINST Too expensive versus rivals
SUM UP Why buy it over a Fabia?

### Golf
FOR Touchy-feely quality materials
AGAINST Suddenly feeling old
SUM UP Still the most sensible private choice

### Bora
FOR Golf with a boot
AGAINST Vigorous depreciation
SUM UP Leave it to the Americans

### Beetle
FOR It's a joke
AGAINST It's on you
SUM UP Fashion is a fickle thing

### Passat
FOR Feels solid, looks good
AGAINST Stodgy to drive, loud engines
SUM UP In its twilight years

### Touareg
FOR Developed with Porsche, most powerful diesel engine ever
AGAINST £50k FOR a VW?
SUM UP Wannabe king of the hill

## Phaeton
FOR High-tech luxury
AGAINST Wrong badge
SUM UP Engineering, engineering, engineering

## Sharan
FOR People carrier, VW badge
AGAINST Old, tired
SUM UP Best considered second hand

## VOLVO
### S40
FOR Tough
AGAINST Horrible
SUM UP You can't kill the buggers

### V40
FOR Estate practicality, chunky good looks
AGAINST Dull chassis, expensive
SUM UP Compact Dutch hearse

### S60
FOR Smooth, soft-edged progress
AGAINST Starts to feel baggy very early on
SUM UP The new age 3-series

### V70
FOR Enormous, safe, Volvo-ish
AGAINST Grey miserable cabin
SUM UP The school-run challenger

### S80
FOR Big, not a BMW, not a Merc
AGAINST Wobbly, thirsty
SUM UP Only if you have to be different

### XC90
FOR Good ride and handling
AGAINST Diesel doesn't suit Geartronic
SUM UP Choose manual or petrol

## WESTFIELD
### Westfield
FOR Fast
AGAINST Flimsy
SUM UP Disposable thrills

## Chapter 17

# Parker's:
## Used & new car Chooser

The amount of information available to used car buyers is increasing, with a number of magazines and guides evaluating cars and providing an indication of values. There are wide variations in the amount paid for new cars because of dealer incentives and variations in trade-in valuations. With used cars, life is even more complicated because each is an individual.

Parker's publishes the private buyer's equivalents to Glass's and CAP Black Book, the guides used by the trade. Parker's used & new car Chooser assesses all cars sold used in Britain. On this, and the following pages, there are summaries (published in spring 2003) from some of the cars featured. Chooser has extensive data and information about used cars and Parker's also provides a price guide. See also Parker's online (www.parkers.co.uk).

### Alfa GTV
FOR Panache; performance
AGAINST There are cheaper choices

**VALUE** ***
Coupe now relatively common, with early cars fairly affordable now; the scarcer soft-top Spider remains quite pricey.

**COSTS** ***
Alfa's dealer network is small, but a network of specialists will work with enthusiasm and skill at lower cost.

**RELIABILITY** ***
No rust worries; frequent minor niggles outnumber major problems; proper maintenance is vital; trim feels flimsy.

**DRIVING** ****
Sharp chassis on both cars; handling is nimble thanks to front-drive layout and accurate steering; Spider flexes at speed but is composed and fluent.

**PERFORMANCE** ****
2.0 Twin Spark sparkles and offers plenty of entertainment; 3.0 V6 sounds wonderful and is seriously quick.

## COMFORT ***
GTV is strictly a 2+2 – rear seats are only for kids; cabin feels cramped; trim is poor for a car at this price; lumpy ride is least of worries in body-flexing Spider.

## IMAGE *****
Exquisite detailing and great engines; these models mark Alfa's return to traditional strengths – style, ability, passion...

## SAFETY ****
Air bags and ABS – reassuring in what can feel a less than solid structure.

## SECURITY ****
Code immobiliser plus remote alarm.

# Audi A6 (1994-97)
FOR Safe; solid; sensibly priced for a quality executive car
AGAINST Less fun to drive than most rivals

## VALUE ***
Good ones are not cheap; even early high-milers retain a quality feel.

## COSTS **
Depreciation has slowed; Audi parts and servicing costly but vital to maintain full history; good fuel economy from TDi.

## RELIABILITY ****
Look after it and it will look after you; high mileage not a problem; rare S6 Turbo and Quattro need specialist care – and it costs.

## DRIVING ***
Steering is better weighted and more precise than the old 100; good grip and stability; strong brakes.

## PERFORMANCE ***
V6 engines match BMW sixes for smooth urgency; S6 is thrusting but controllable; turbo-diesel models do their stuff with little fuss – try the surprising TDi 140.

## COMFORT ****
Spacious, airy cabin; excellent layout; estates very roomy; some wind noise.

## IMAGE ***
Durable as lederhosen; for people who value substance and lasting quality.

## SAFETY ****
Strong body incorporates clever safety features; airbag and ABS for additional assurance.

## SECURITY ****
Immobiliser, alarm, plus good locks.

# BMW 3-Series (1991-98)
FOR Image; smooth six-cylinder engines; great to drive
AGAINST Not much standard equipment; limited rear legroom; less exclusive than some rivals

## VALUE ****
Prices are falling faster now, especially for earliest cars; avoid under-equipped ex-fleet 316i and 318i; six cylinder cars with SE spec are favoured – sunroof, alloys and metallic paint are all liked.

## COSTS ***
Main agent servicing costs high – best to use cheaper independent specialists after the first three or four years within the BMW network; that said, insist on BMW parts – 'pattern' parts are usually a false economy.

## RELIABILITY ****
Some quality niggles in the early years but few significant faults; the most serious are valve problems which can kill engines.

## DRIVING *****
Great chassis invites being driven hard; excellent driving position; slick gear change; smooth, willing engines; it all adds up to give real driver satisfaction.

## PERFORMANCE ****
316i and 318i are only workmanlike; 1.9 16-valve and 2.8 are smooth; 2.0 is the best all-round choice; 325tds turbo-diesel is surprisingly accomplished for an oil-burner – and frugal, too.

### COMFORT ****
Excellent in the front; well-designed and generously sized seats, nice dashboard; low noise levels though sporty models have a firm ride; just a bit restricted for rear occupants.

### IMAGE ****
Desirable, dynamic, but its message is not subtle; democratisation of BMW's image means 3-Series lacks exclusivity.

### SAFETY ***
Reasonably safe overall; ABS from 1992, driver's airbag from Oct 93; passenger airbag on later Compact models; optional side airbags on latest cars.

### SECURITY ****
Visible VIN numbers; good immobilisers fitted from 1992, plus deadlocks on six-cylinder cars.

## BMW 5-Series (1996-2003)
FOR Understated elegance; engines; driving pleasure
AGAINST Little chance of finding a bargain

### VALUE ****
No cheap ones – £10,000 only buys you the earliest 520i – but feel the quality; values are holding quite well.

### COSTS ***
Costly BMW servicing is a must; fuel economy is good for a big car – 30 mpg from 520i/525i, nearly 40 from 530d.

### RELIABILITY *****
It would be surprising if anything went amiss; many are under warranty.

### DRIVING *****
Poised handling, precise steering; supple chassis gives a fine ride; tidy handling is always confident and controlled but slightly tame compared to the 3-series; Sport versions have a tauter chassis.

### PERFORMANCE *****
Effortless acceleration from all except 520i – bigger engines feel languid as they deliver swift progress; V8 is vocal when pushed; all are refined at speed; 525d and 530d are remarkable engines.

### COMFORT *****
Spacious cabin offers more room in rear than formerly; big seats are a bit flat; luxury environment; bigger boot.

### IMAGE *****
Difficult to fault and distinctive enough to project an impression; subtle in metallic silver – the colour of money.

### SAFETY *****
ABS; strong body; twin airbags, with side airbags from Sept 96; improved again in late 1997; top marks for Euro NCAP crash tests.

### SECURITY *****
Alarm and effective immobiliser; a thief is very unlikely to be able to drive away.

## BMW 7-Series (1994-2002)
FOR Performance; refinement
AGAINST Running costs

### VALUE ****
Getting on a bit and just replaced, but a superb used car for the money.

### COSTS **
Very high servicing and parts costs, but the biggest financial hit is depreciation.

### RELIABILITY ****
Needs proper maintenance to ensure reliability; possible electronics gremlins.

### DRIVING *****
Suspension irons out every little bump; perfect road manners yet it can also be exciting; approaching the ultimate.

### PERFORMANCE *****
2.8 is powerful enough for most; all are strong and smooth; the V8s are tremendous; the V12 is great but superfluous.

## COMFORT *****
Sumptuous cabin, cosseting seats; quiet, smooth ride; rear legroom is adequate in standard cabin, generous in LWB cars.

## IMAGE ***
Fading a little due to the arrival of the latest S-class and its own successor, but still redolent of plutocratic power.

## SAFETY ****
ABS; twin airbags; head airbags from Sept 97; optional rear side airbags on recent cars.

## SECURITY *****
Alarm and immobiliser; lock shielding is much improved from last generation; these measures seem most effective.

# Chrysler Voyager/GrandVoyager (1997-2001)
FOR Very roomy; loads of equipment
AGAINST US-style thirst; poor crash test results

## VALUE ****
Generous standard equipment; reasonable prices; holding its value quite well.

## COSTS **
3.3 and 2.0 Auto are thirsty; parts and servicing are dear; insurance is high.

## RELIABILITY *****
Should be very reliable if correctly serviced; tough and durable.

## DRIVING ***
Steering feels remote; ride is a bit fidgety; 3.3 is the most relaxing drive.

## PERFORMANCE **
2.0 feels underpowered and sluggish; 3.3 a good cruiser; engines a bit coarse.

## COMFORT ****
Very roomy, especially Grand Voyager; flexible seating layouts but awkward to rearrange; generous load space.

## IMAGE ****
Voyager is to North America what the Espace is to Europe — original, stylish, practical and desirable.

## SAFETY ***
ABS; twin airbags; construction appears solid but Voyager got very poor ratings in Euro NCAP crash testing.

## SECURITY ***
Standard immobiliser.

# Citroen C5
FOR Space; comfort; 2.0 HDi performance
AGAINST Steering and brakes lack feel

## VALUE ****
Specifications are generous across the range; depreciation is steep but not that much worse than fleet/family contenders like Primera, 406 and Laguna.

## COSTS ***
Competitive fuel economy from all engines especially the common rail diesel units; long service intervals.

## RELIABILITY ***
Because the car is so new, the jury is still out on this — but the old Xantia was frequently plagued by minor faults.

## DRIVING ****
The 'Hydractive' suspension has two modes on Executive models, normal or sport; handling is safe and secure, though not as sharp as the current Passat or Mondeo; good body control.

## PERFORMANCE ****
1.8 16v petrol unit is modestly capable; 2.0 16v and HPi units feel fast; 3.0 V6 is more of a cruiser than a sporting machine; 2.2 HDi is the pick of the diesels, with plenty of torque even though it's not very high revving.

## COMFORT *****
Hydractive suspension provides a very supple ride; front seats are very comfortable with generous all-ways adjustment, but the driving position is not as good as rivals; rear space is excellent with a useful rear armrest and

ski hatch; huge boot, and the estate is cavernous.

### IMAGE ***
Possibly the weakest link besides the daft name is the styling – it looks handsome from some angles but odd from others; radical but idiosyncratic.

### SAFETY ****
Strong bodyshell helped C5 to gain four stars on Euro NCAP crash test; standard ABS and airbags on all versions.

### SECURITY ****
A transponder immobiliser is standard on all models, with Exclusive models also benefiting from an alarm.

## Daewoo Matiz
FOR Style; space; equipment
AGAINST Puny engine

### VALUE *****
Generous equipment for little money; three-year/60,000 mile warranty and free servicing for first three years.

### COSTS *****
Free servicing deal reduces running costs; very good fuel economy; low insurance; depreciation is not too steep.

### RELIABILITY ****
Daewoo have a good reputation for reliability; the warranty and servicing deal means all should be well maintained; long-term build quality is unproven.

### DRIVING ***
Excellent all-round vision; user-friendly; pedals rather small and close-set; light and easy steering for nipping about town.

### PERFORMANCE **
Underpowered – needs hard revving to get sufficient acceleration; hills and overtaking are a struggle, especially when fully laden; copes adequately once it builds up to cruising speed.

### COMFORT ***
Pleasant cabin; generous headroom; rear

legroom restricted; flexible stowage facilities; good ride for such a small car.

### IMAGE ***
Cheerful and cheeky-looking with bags of character; bargain basement but it's cheap chic at just half the price of a Mercedes A-Class.

### SAFETY ****
Twin airbags are standard; stability at speed as good as any other small but tall car – it would take a very reckless manoeuvre to upset the Matiz; three-star rating for the Euro NCAP crash test.

### SECURITY ***
Factory-fitted immobiliser but no alarm; extra precautions advisable.

## Daihatsu Fourtrak
FOR Sturdy; long lived
AGAINST Poor on-road ride

### VALUE ****
Tough, practical, capable and versatile; excellent off-road or for light towing.

### COSTS ***
Fuel-efficient diesels; reasonable parts and servicing; short service intervals.

### RELIABILITY ****
Rugged engines; good build quality; will last to high mileages with care.

### DRIVING ***
Selectable 4WD; easy to manoeuvre; firm ride with some body roll.

### PERFORMANCE **
2.0 pulls well, 2.8 TD is gutsy; both are noisy and slow; capable in the rough.

### COMFORT **
Base models spartan; small load space.

### IMAGE **
Respected as a rural workhorse.

### SAFETY **
No ABS or airbags; sturdy build.

**SECURITY** *
Immobiliser on Independent SE.

## Fiat Multipla
FOR Clever design; good ride
AGAINST Looks; width

### VALUE ****
Clever six-seater compact MPV beats both
Vauxhall Zafira and Renault Scenic on
specification and price.

### COSTS ****
Good fuel consumption, especially from JTD;
long service intervals keep running costs
down; holding its value a bit better than
most other Fiats.

### RELIABILITY ***
Too early to say, but Fiat has not done well in
reliability surveys; build quality is OK but
regular maintenance will be vital.

### DRIVING ***
Multipla's width takes some getting used to
– watch out for those width-restricted
residential streets; otherwise easy to drive;
all-round visibility is good.

### PERFORMANCE ***
Engines are both adequate; go for the
common rail JTD turbo-diesel if economy and
more torque are wanted.

### COMFORT *****
Innovative seating opts for two rows of three
seats; light aluminium chairs can be removed
easily and rearranged in various
configurations; composed ride.

### IMAGE ****
Awkward-looking Multipla may be, but it's a
definite head-turner; is it cool or just too
weird for cautious British buyers?

### SAFETY ****
ABS on all models; driver and passenger
airbags with side airbags option; three stars
for the Euro NCAP crash test.

**SECURITY** ***
Fiat code immobiliser is standard, plus an
alarm on ELX models, but extra precautions
might be a sensible idea.

## Ford Fiesta (1995-99)
FOR Lively 16-valve engines; much improved
ride and refinement
AGAINST Not enough room for rear
passengers or luggage

### VALUE ***
Not best value in class when new, but used
prices have tumbled because of high
volumes; Encore models have rather miserly
equipment.

### COSTS ****
Good fuel economy, inexpensive parts, and
10,000-mile service intervals all contribute
to low running costs.

### RELIABILITY ****
Very good so far apart from niggling minor
electrical faults; 16-valve engines need
careful servicing to avoid problems.

### DRIVING *****
Go for the nippy, refined 16-valve cars; avoid
the 1.8 diesel. Precise steering and good
grip make it fun to drive.

### PERFORMANCE ****
1.3 is merely adequate; 1.4 16-valve is
worth the extra for its acceleration
advantage, though the 1.25 is also
responsive; Auto versions are rather
sluggish.

### COMFORT ***
Ride is a huge improvement on earlier
Fiestas; noise levels are down too; quite
refined, though the rear seat is rather
cramped and load space could be better.

### IMAGE ***
Classiest Fiesta yet looks fairly modern, with
curvy, youthful styling, though it's less radical
than its funky little sister, Ka.

### SAFETY ***
Three stars for the Euro NCAP crash test; driver's airbag and effective seat belts; optional anti-lock brakes.

### SECURITY ****
One of the best protected small cars around, with strong locks, visible VIN plate and immobiliser; alarm on Ghia models.

## Ford Focus
FOR Bold styling and packaging; handling
AGAINST Too radical for some; will soon be as common as the Escort

### VALUE ****
Priced to appeal to fleet buyers as well as private motorists; option packs mean you only buy the equipment that you want; well equipped, well engineered; used ones are getting cheaper, with lots of Zetec and LX cars about.

### COSTS ****
Low Ford running costs; good fuel economy; holding its value reasonably well; affordable parts and servicing.

### RELIABILITY ****
Build quality looks good and reliability is above-average; some minor problems.

### DRIVING *****
Very driver-friendly – agile and easy to handle, allowing even less confident drivers to feel secure; always enjoyable yet surprisingly forgiving.

### PERFORMANCE ****
1.4 and 1.8 TDi diesel are a bit sluggish; newer TDCi is better; Zetec 1.6 and 1.8 are lively – 1.8 is most flexible; 2.0 is brisk; speed freaks will relish the ST170 and the startlingly fast RS model.

### COMFORT ****
Spacious with a well-designed cabin and user-friendly control layout; smooth refined ride; flexible and practical for all the family; seats could do with more lumbar support.

### IMAGE ***
Focus's 'New Edge' lines are modern, efficient but no longer different – due to over-familiarity. But even though Focus is such a common sight, familiarity does not breed contempt – it's well packaged, well executed and well regarded.

### SAFETY ****
Exceeds class standards all round; incorporates the latest modern crash safety features; near the top of its class with a four-star rating for the Euro NCAP crash test.

### SECURITY ****
One of the best cars in the class for beating thieves; bonnet lock; double-locking doors; immobiliser; other security and alarm options are available from Ford dealers.

## Ford Mondeo (1993-2000)
FOR Well designed; easy to own; satisfying to drive
AGAINST Some shabby cars about now

### VALUE ****
Britain's most popular fleet car, so lots about at very competitive prices; aim for LX spec or better – and be very choosy.

### COSTS ****
Fleet operator requirements keep servicing and parts costs under control, but labour times for repairs are longer than for old technology Fords – clutches in particular are costly to fix.

### RELIABILITY ****
Fundamentally reliable despite some localised failures.

### DRIVING ****
Rewarding to drive, poised and precise; inspires confidence – especially the much revised models from 1996.

### PERFORMANCE ***
1.8 is lively enough and fairly economical; 1.8 turbo-diesel is steady but not very refined; 2.0 is willing but a bit gruff; V6 is sensational and smooth.

**COMFORT** ****
Good visibility, perfect driving position; nice switchgear; rear seat is just about adequate for adults; estates are roomy.

**IMAGE** **
Mundane Mondeo, beloved of rep fleets everywhere; facelifted cars from 1996 look fresher and more distinctive.

**SAFETY** **
Side impact beams, driver's airbag; now below average in class, with 2.5 stars in NCAP crash test for the improved 1997 model; ABS standard on many by 1995.

**SECURITY** **
Anti-theft alarm; effective immobiliser except on early cars; weak door locks.

## Honda Civic (2000 on)
FOR Interior space; equipment
AGAINST Odd looks

**VALUE** ****
Competitively priced and well equipped for the money; residual values are firm.

**COSTS** ***
Good fuel economy; insurance groups are comparable to rivals; service costs tend to be higher than average for class.

**RELIABILITY** ****
Too new to tell, but previous Civic models are acclaimed for their reliability.

**DRIVING** ****
Precise handling from a balanced chassis; electric power assisted steering is light and accurate; pleasingly sporty.

**PERFORMANCE** ****
Engines are tuned for driving flexibility; 1.4 is the sweetest and loves revs; 1.6 VTEC has more torque; latest generation 1.7i engine in the Coupe needs revving hard to get the best out of it; Type-R is amazingly brisk and free-revving.

**COMFORT** ****
Leg- and head-room are exceptional – tall people travel in comfort, in front or rear.

Well designed cabin; dash-mounted gear shift gives extra space between the front seats, creating a 'walk-through' interior.

**IMAGE** ***
Fresh and innovative, clean and purposeful; sporty Type-R lifts its credibility as a fast Focus rival.

**SAFETY** ****
ABS with electronic brakeforce distribution (EBD); front and side airbags; Honda predicts a four star Euro NCAP rating.

**SECURITY** ****
Immobiliser, keyless entry and deadlocks; SE/Executive also have an alarm.

## Honda Legend
FOR Equipment; refinement
AGAINST Poor economy; sloppy handling; lacks image

**VALUE** ***
Virtually everything is standard, including a two-year warranty; Honda's reputation for reliability is a bonus, too; what kills Legend's appeal is that it lacks prestige; impact of depreciation makes it a far cheaper but less desirable choice than its nearest rival, the Lexus LS 400.

**COSTS** **
Unimpressive fuel economy is a minor problem compared with plummeting depreciation; Legend is really only worth considering if you find a nice cheap early '90s car or the company is paying.

**RELIABILITY** *****
At the top of its class – after all, it's a Honda; this top of the range saloon is very unlikely to leave you stranded.

**DRIVING** ***
Handling is competent enough, but hard cornering brings loss of grip and noticeable body roll; makes some sense as a US-style luxury cruiser.

### PERFORMANCE ***

Smooth power delivery from the V6 engines – although this is best experienced in a straight line; refined unless pushed very hard.

### COMFORT ***

Lots of room inside, especially in the back; drawbacks are some road noise on poor surfaces and ride that's too firm at lower speeds; mechanically refined, but cannot match its luxury rivals.

### IMAGE **

Lexus scored with image-conscious British buyers, but Legend almost missed the game; in the rarefied luxury car market, cars need to be noticed – and Legend is all too easily overlooked.

### SAFETY ****

Legend is large and feels very safe; driver and passenger airbags, ABS and seat belt pre-tensioners as standard on later models, but no side airbags or traction control until 1999.

### SECURITY ***

Immobiliser, alarm and remote central locking are all standard.

## Hyundai Santa Fe

FOR Well equipped; easy to drive
AGAINST Thirsty petrol engines; odd styling; poor gearchange

### VALUE ****

A Discovery-sized 4x4 for Freelander money and the overall package is very tempting; equipment levels are high and there's an excellent warranty; future residual values are only average.

### COSTS ***

10,000-mile service intervals; parts and service costs are reasonable; petrol engines are thirsty, diesel gives 35 mpg.

### RELIABILITY ****

Other models in the Hyundai range are known for their dependability, and Santa Fe should be no different; build quality is better than on older Hyundai models.

### DRIVING ***

Feels nimble to drive despite its bulky shape; steering is light; all-round visibility is generally good; if pushed harder, the handling starts to feel less stable.

### PERFORMANCE ****

2.4 is refined and offers acceptable performance; V6 is smooth and powerful; 2.0 turbo-diesel is noticeably slower to pick up speed but pulls well and is at its best when cruising.

### COMFORT ****

Seats are supportive but the driver's seat position is either too upright or laid back; steering wheel is adjustable for rake but not reach. Spacious, with plenty of room for rear passengers.

### IMAGE ***

It's certainly eye-catching, with curvy styling that is reminiscent of other popular 4x4 models; big, striking but perhaps a touch tacky.

### SAFETY ****

All models benefit from standard ABS, with EBD (Electronic Brakeforce Distribution); driver and passenger airbags; beat the Forester, Wrangler, Cherokee, RAV-4, CR-V and the latest generation Maverick in US crash tests.

### SECURITY ***

An alarm and immobiliser are standard; might be worth considering upgrading the security equipment in urban areas.

## Jaguar XJ Series (1994 on)

FOR Massive power; deluxe comfort
AGAINST Punishing running costs

### VALUE ****

Years of refinement have brought the XJ to perfect pitch, though the standards have been raised by newer rivals; all models have every refinement.

### COSTS *

Very expensive to buy, run, insure and maintain; original six- and twelve- cylinder cars are cheap but devalued by the arrival of the V8 in 1998; depreciation will always be very heavy.

### RELIABILITY ****
No major faults, but regular specialist servicing is essential; despite huge improvements, build quality is still not quite up to German standards.

### DRIVING *****
Absolutely obedient and graceful, though steering could provide better feedback; handling and balance compare favourably with smaller sports cars.

### PERFORMANCE *****
Massive torque; 370 bhp XJR is extraordinarily fast for its weight; all are quieter than before, powerful but poised; latest V8 is great teamed with the new five-speed auto, whether you choose the smaller 3.2 or the creamy 4.0.

### COMFORT ****
Cabin is even more luxurious than before; rear accommodation is better than formerly but still not as spacious as S-Class or Lexus.

### IMAGE ***
Retro-classic but misses the mark compared with latest 7-Series or S-Class.

### SAFETY *****
ABS; twin airbags; side airbags and automatic electronic stability control from Sept 97; 4.0 has traction control.

### SECURITY ****
Alarm and immobiliser system; later cars are more secure, with shielded deadlocks.

## Jeep Cherokee (1993-2001)
FOR Tough and well equipped
AGAINST Running costs

### VALUE ***
A versatile alternative to a family estate; used prices are falling faster now.

### COSTS **
Thirsty – even the 2.5 turbo-diesel; parts and servicing costs are a bit steep.

### RELIABILITY ****
Generally excellent, but high milers or towing vehicles can suffer expensively.

### DRIVING ***
Easy to drive; nimble; quite refined.

### PERFORMANCE ****
4.0 is athletic with brisk acceleration; 2.5 TD is more sedate but adequate.

### COMFORT ***
Cosseting seats; adequate luggage area; interior of early cars looks old-fashioned.

### IMAGE ***
Cherokee is still likeable, but it's showing its age beside newer rivals.

### SAFETY ***
ABS on all 4.0 models; driver's airbag from 1994; passenger airbag standard on 4.0 from '94, on rest from March '97.

### SECURITY **
Alarm on most but immobiliser on latest models only; could use more protection.

## Kia Sedona
FOR Comfort; value for money
AGAINST Indifferent build quality; heavy depreciation

### VALUE ****
Masses of space and equipment at very tempting prices, although top versions look less attractive when pitched against rivals such as Mitsubishi Space Wagon. Depreciation is turning out to be fairly steep, so it's most sensible to buy a used example.

### COSTS ***
Choose the diesel if fuel economy is a priority – 2.5 V6 is thirsty, particularly in auto mode; reasonable parts and servicing costs.

### RELIABILITY ***
Hyundai's past performance suggests that the engine and drivetrain should be durable enough; however build quality is only so-so, especially inside; with the punishing usage a family MPV is likely to get, this could lead to plenty of minor faults.

### DRIVING ***
Although it's big and van-like, Sedona is an easy MPV to drive with the auto 'box; although it's reasonably nimble in town, it's at its best as a motorway cruiser.

### PERFORMANCE ***
V6 is not exactly fast but its responses are lusty enough to keep the driver in a hurry happy. The original 2.9 turbo-diesel is a bit of a plodder, taking over 17 seconds for the 0-60 mph sprint; the more powerful CRDi launched in late 2001 is noticeably brisker.

### COMFORT *****
Extremely spacious with a useful 'walk-through' area between the front two rows of seats. Seating is versatile with comfortable armchairs that swivel around on original version (though they can't be removed). Rear seats are removable on later cars. There's even separate air conditioning in the rear.

### IMAGE ***
This brash MPV could be mistaken for a Voyager from a distance. Space, comfort and value are attractive but so-so quality and Kia badge may deter some buyers.

### SAFETY ***
Driver and front passenger airbags are standard; ABS on SX models upwards; all models have side impact protection bars.

### SECURITY **
Immobiliser on all models but no alarm – this is a serious omission in this class.

## Land Rover Freelander
FOR The badge; frugal Td4 diesel; off-road ability
AGAINST Thirsty V6; quite expensive to buy

### VALUE ****
Balance of road manners and off-road ability; five-door Station Wagon is the family choice; Softback is more macho.

### COSTS ***
1.8 petrol and the refined BMW-sourced Td4 diesel are the economy choices; is holding its value quite well.

### RELIABILITY **
Current models feel better built and more solidly engineered than their predecessors; older Freelanders have a reputation for problems, mainly minor but niggling.

### DRIVING ****
Stable, well-controlled ride; quite nimble and car-like to drive; both the V6 and Td4 are very smooth and refined.

### PERFORMANCE ****
All Freelander models are excellent on the motorway and in town; V6 is the performance choice, but the Td4 is the better overall package; Hill Descent Control makes up for lack of dual-ratio gearbox.

### COMFORT ****
Some of the switchgear is very poorly placed and of variable quality; the driving position feels compromised for taller drivers; the front seats feel short of both height and length; five-door estate models have the most rear legroom.

### IMAGE ****
Blend of Land Rover heritage with curvy modern looks. Chunky at the front, nicely finished at the back; most convincing as a three-door Softback, but the five-door Station Wagon works well too.

### SAFETY ***
Driver's airbag standard on all models; passenger airbag on XS, GS and ES models; ABS was an expensive option on cheaper models at launch but is now standard across the range.

### SECURITY ****
Alarm and immobiliser are standard; no reports yet regarding their effectiveness, but it may be worth increasing protection for town use.

## Lexus LS (1990-2000)
FOR All-round abilities; beats rivals on price
AGAINST Keen drivers may be disappointed

### VALUE *****
Better value than GS300; a worthy rival to 7-Series, A8 or S-Class if you're not after the ultimate driving experience.

## COSTS ***
Undercuts the Germans considerably and is cheaper to run and maintain; however, it's still no paragon of frugality.

## RELIABILITY *****
Excellent reliability, though regular servicing is vital; build quality is superb but it doesn't feel as solid as the A8.

## DRIVING ****
Supple suspension is even better after revisions in 1993; steering sharper than an XJ Jaguar but still a little vague; all-round handling is impressive.

## PERFORMANCE *****
Sprightly, with good aerodynamics; rapid, silently surging acceleration; delivers plenty of power with no fuss.

## COMFORT ***
Roomy interior aims for opulence but falls short – leather, wood and switches feel cheap; top-notch audio kit, though.

## IMAGE ***
Less sleek and more overt in its opulence than GS300; a bit of a bosses' barge – far too flashy for 'old money'.

## SAFETY ****
ABS; twin airbags from Jan 1993; Vehicle Stability Control from Jan 1998.

## SECURITY ***
Alarm and immobiliser; as with any luxury car, a tracking system would be a sensible investment.

## Mazda MX-5
**FOR** Classic modern roadster; affordable
**AGAINST** Cheap Eunos imports without history

## VALUE ***
Still desirable but getting cheaper as 'grey' Eunos imports depress prices.

## COSTS ***
Only genuine UK cars hold their value; reasonable running and maintenance costs; plenty of independent specialists.

## RELIABILITY ****
Very reliable if used sensibly; some problems with pop-up headlamps; avoid tarted-up write-offs or thrashed rubbish with no history from Japan.

## DRIVING ****
One of the best fun sportsters; precise handling and well-balanced; upgraded 1.8 is pokier but heavier to drive.

## PERFORMANCE ****
Original 1.6 is a little underpowered – 1.8i is best; all afford lots of driver enjoyment although they lack real muscle.

## COMFORT ****
User-friendly hood and tonneau cover; good sports seats; well-styled retro dash; basic models are rather spartan.

## IMAGE *****
Youthful, classless, affordable and fun-loving; a modern car with retro charm that kicked off the '90s roadster revival; probably a future collectable.

## SAFETY ***
ABS on some; side impact protection beams 1993; driver's airbag on 1.8iS; four-star NCAP rating for 2002 model.

## SECURITY ***
Immobiliser on some; get an alarm.

## Mazda Xedos 6
**FOR** Good looks; smooth V6 engine; build quality
**AGAINST** Cramped cabin

## VALUE ***
A viable alternative to an A4 or 3-Series in terms of ability but lacks prestige in this company; elegant styling.

## COSTS ***
Reasonable servicing and parts costs; high insurance; fuel economy is not bad for a V6; depreciation quite high; some end-of-line cars are still under warranty.

## RELIABILITY ****
Mazda have a great reliability record but

service history is vital on high-mileage ex-fleet cars; some minor electrical niggles on hard-worked cars.

### DRIVING ***
Very competent handling; safe and stable but steering is far too light; pedals are offset and slightly awkward; not an all-out driving machine like a BMW.

### PERFORMANCE ***
1.6 lacks real punch and is rendered otiose by the fine V6; Auto is smooth and responsive; a pleasing all-rounder.

### COMFORT ***
Rear is cramped; low roofline restricts headroom; boot is on the small side but split rear seat increases practicality; good seats and a comfy ride.

### IMAGE ***
Reasonably discreet though V6 gives it some kudos; curvy shape is attractive to some; subtle and sensible.

### SAFETY ***
Driver's airbag from 1994; ABS; well built and solid enough, but not outstanding.

### SECURITY ***
Simple and effective transponder code immobiliser from March 95; remote locking available; really needs an alarm.

## Mercedes E-Class (1995-2002)
FOR Prestige; longevity; integrity; low depreciation
AGAINST Most expensive choice in the class

### VALUE ****
You'll never regret buying quality; a good long-term prospect; fully equipped Elegance and Avantgarde models are preferred to the basic Classic.

### COSTS ***
Depreciates slowly, so long-term costs work out lower than for lesser rivals whose values plunge faster; big bills for routine maintenance and servicing but it pays off; fuel consumption is rather high, except for diesels – 220 CDi gives over 40 mpg; insurance premiums are high.

### RELIABILITY *****
No significant problems; just keep the M-B history up to date and your E-Class should run to very high mileages; build integrity is pretty well unrivalled; very solid.

### DRIVING ****
Supple suspension, taut chassis, precisely weighted steering; safe, silken smooth progress; on the heavy side, but doesn't feel particularly unwieldy.

### PERFORMANCE ****
Rapid acceleration from six-cylinder cars; very quiet and relaxed at speed; auto 'box gives seamless changes; diesels are strong but four-cylinder engines not really adequate; AMG models are fabulous.

### COMFORT *****
Roomy interior front and rear; supportive seats; excellent quality trim with proper wood finishes; big deep boot; creamy ride; very low noise levels; all the gadgets possibly needed; is there a more comfortable executive car?

### IMAGE *****
Meets the aspirations of most buyers in this class and whispers success more discreetly than a BMW 5-Series; this big Merc looks modern, not monolithic; the estates wed practicality and prestige.

### SAFETY ****
Four stars for Euro NCAP crash tests; superb structural integrity; lots of safety features – ABS, traction control, twin airbags, plus side bags from June 1996.

### SECURITY ****
Alarm, effective immobiliser, visible VIN – but no deadlocks? Desirable to thieves, so it needs extra Thatcham-approved protection – or fit a tracking system.

## Mercedes S-Class (1991-99)

FOR Pedigree; quality; engineering
AGAINST Size; sky-high running costs; 'fat cat' image

### VALUE ****
Obsolete but still retains some prestige; monster depreciation – so buy a mid-90s example for best value.

### COSTS *
Horrendous; sheds value rapidly; thirsty; big bills for servicing at M-B dealerships.

### RELIABILITY *****
Superb, but full M-B service history is a must; electronic faults are a possibility; build quality is unparalleled; capable of huge mileages; usually well cared for.

### DRIVING *****
Surprisingly agile despite its bulk; stable and perfectly balanced under all conditions; very impressive.

### PERFORMANCE ****
Not quite as nippy as the 7-Series, even in 'sport' mode, but very potent; V8 engines are smoother than the sixes; very swift – even the monster Limo.

### COMFORT *****
Palatial, sumptuous accommodation; leather and materials exquisite; seats are almost infinitely adjustable.

### IMAGE ***
Bloated boardroom Panzer; a trophy car – ownership often had more to do with the appearance of wealth than taste or environmental awareness.

### SAFETY ****
Massive structure; ABS; twin airbags; side airbags June 1996; acceleration skid control on larger-engined models.

### SECURITY ***
Alarm and immobiliser; revised models are more secure; many have sophisticated after-market systems, including satellite trackers.

## MGF and TF

FOR Styling; handling; brand heritage
AGAINST Dated interior; patchy build quality

### VALUE ***
Launch of MG TF has brought MGF prices down. MG TF is well equipped except for the basic 115. Options are expensive.

### COSTS ***
Relatively cheap to run, with OK fuel consumption and affordable parts costs.

### RELIABILITY ***
Early MGFs were often poorly finished; later cars usually OK if properly serviced.

### DRIVING ***
MGF has good handling but the body flexes and shakes; MGTF rides more firmly and is a more rewarding drive.

### PERFORMANCE ****
Free-revving twin-cam engines are willing and responsive; 1.6i is adequate; 1.8i is lively; tweaked VVC is swift; gearbox is a bit notchy; steering is on the heavy side.

### COMFORT ***
Parts bin interior is MGF's weak point; MG TF is better but still dated; good seats but cramped for tall people.

### IMAGE ****
True sports roadsters worthy of the MG badge; TF freshens up the offering.

### SAFETY ***
Old fashioned chassis but meets all modern criteria; no Euro NCAP results; ABS is only optional on some models.

### SECURITY ****
Immobiliser, alarm and deadlocks, plus visible VIN.

## MINI
FOR Slick handling; cool image
AGAINST Poor rear space

### VALUE ****
Competitively priced with generous
equipment. Vast array of options allows
scope for personalisation.

### COSTS ****
Over 40 mpg; minimal depreciation so far;
insurance is competitive; just £100 buys five
years' free servicing from new.

### RELIABILITY ***
Built in England, BMW-designed, with
engines from South America. Build quality is
generally high but early models suffered
some niggling faults.

### DRIVING *****
Precise steering with plenty of feedback;
body control is excellent and suspension is
sportily firm; grip and roadholding are good
(best on optional 16-inch alloys). Engaging
and reminiscent of the original, but far more
refined and sophisticated.

### PERFORMANCE ***
All models use a DaimlerChrysler 1.6 litre
engine; performance is adequate in One and
Cooper but both need to be worked hard;
supercharged Cooper S picks up quickly and
performs strongly throughout the rev range.

### COMFORT ***
Low-slung driving position feels sporty; front
head- and leg-room are excellent but rear
accommodation is no better than the
cramped original Mini, and the rear seat
bench is hard and unsupportive; less load
space than many superminis.

### IMAGE *****
'Must have' fashion accessory – chic,
modern and desirable. Strongly evocative –
retro in both ironic and iconic senses.

### SAFETY ****
Strong body; driver, passenger and side
airbags; ABS with electronic braking
distribution (EBD) plus optional traction
control; four-star NCAP crash test rating.

### SECURITY ***
Immobiliser and remote central locking;
alarm is an option on One and Cooper.
Tracker might be a worthwhile option.

## Mitsubishi Space Wagon (1998 on)
FOR Easy to drive; punchy GDI engine
AGAINST Less elegant than some rivals

### VALUE ****
Practical seven-seater family wheels at a
sensible price; generous equipment, too.

### COSTS ****
GDI direct-injection petrol unit gives fair fuel
economy; reliability will keep costs down; too
early to predict resale values.

### RELIABILITY *****
Previous Space Wagons have stood up well
to heavy family use; well built.

### DRIVING ****
Surprisingly agile and easy to drive; the
driving position is commanding though rather
upright; all-round vision is good.

### PERFORMANCE ****
2.4 engine has good mid-range pull, feels
lively and cruises comfortably; 2.0 is
adequate for most types of driving.

### COMFORT ****
Ride is a bit ragged when pushed hard, with
some roll; easy access to rear seats thanks
to sliding middle row; space inside rivals
Galaxy and Sharan.

### IMAGE ***
Fashionable family MPV, but Space Wagon is
a bit too boxy and van-like to be a real style
statement; practical and pragmatic rather
than posey.

### SAFETY ****
Driver and passenger airbags, plus side
airbags on the GLS; ABS except on the GL;
modern design incorporates strong
structural safety features.

### SECURITY ****
Alarm and immobiliser are standard, but
there are no deadlocks.

## Nissan Terrano

FOR Keenly priced; family-sized interior
AGAINST So-so ride; so-so styling

**VALUE** ***
Versatile; sensible new prices and
cheaper to buy used than class rivals.

**COSTS** ***
Average fuel consumption for class; no
shocks with parts or service costs.

**RELIABILITY** ***
Generally good; interior trim fit is poor and
gets tatty quickly; neglected turbo-diesels
can suffer at high mileages.

**DRIVING** ***
Easy to manoeuvre; steering is a bit vague;
good grip and roadholding; ride is rather
jarring; switchable 4WD.

**PERFORMANCE** ***
Acceleration unimpressive from 2.7 TD
—later TDi is better, and new 3.0 Di is quite
lively; petrol 2.4i is no sprinter either; relaxed
when cruising.

**COMFORT** ***
Supportive seats; dull interior; good load
capacity; 2.7 TD engine is rather noisy
though cabin is well insulated.

**IMAGE** **
Rather plain but practical for family use;
some special editions are a bit tacky.

**SAFETY** **
ABS optional on all from July 1996,
standard on SR Sport, latest SE and SE
Touring; driver's airbag from July 1996.

**SECURITY** *
Poor on early models; alarm and immobiliser
on most from July 1996.

## Peugeot 307

FOR Build quality; excellent ride; safety
equipment
AGAINST Steering lacks feel; petrol model
lacks refinement

**VALUE** ****
Feels well built, and all except the basic cars
are well equipped; still in fairly short supply
on the secondhand market, so values are
likely to remain steady for a while; glass-
roofed SW compact MPV is a credible rival
to Scenic and Zafira.

**COSTS** ****
Good fuel economy, especially from the
frugal diesel models; long service intervals;
parts and servicing costs are reasonable.

**RELIABILITY** ****
Build quality is much improved over the 306;
correct servicing will be very important to
assure reliability.

**DRIVING** ***
Taut responses and reasonable dynamic
ability, plus good body control; steering is
light and not as communicative as 306;
some drivers find it hard to get comfortable;
too much clutch pedal travel.

**PERFORMANCE** ***
All petrol engines are fairly lively, but a little
unrefined; diesel models are both frugal and
fun to drive, especially the D-Turbo; smaller
units are hindered by the 307's substantial
bodyweight.

**COMFORT** ***
The 307 feels unsettled at low speeds and
the ride is poor; rear headroom is a bit
meagre for such a tall car; front and rear
legroom are excellent; rear load area is
capacious and deep, although access is
compromised by the large rear light clusters.

**IMAGE** ****
Looks like a grown-up 206 crossed with an
MPV; smart yet subtle, and unlikely to date
for some time to come.

**SAFETY** ****
All models have six airbags including front
and rear curtain bags; standard ABS with
EBFD (Electronic Brake Force Distribution);
four stars in Euro NCAP test means 307 is
near top in its class.

### SECURITY ***
Effective immobiliser and deadlocks
from Rapier models upwards; alarm with
remote control central locking and deadlocks
are only standard on the XSI and D-Turbo.

## Porsche Boxster
FOR Affordable – for a Porsche; handling;
style
AGAINST High used prices

### VALUE ****
Relatively cheap for a Porsche but with all
qualities intact; no bargains, but little
depreciation; very expensive options.

### COSTS ***
Half the price of a 911 both to buy and
service; labour rates and parts typically
expensive as is insurance; fuel consumption is quite reasonable.

### RELIABILITY *****
Porsche's reputation for reliability won't be
cheapened by this 'cheap' model; some
recalls so far, but nothing serious.

### DRIVING *****
Beautifully balanced; well-designed
cockpit; superb composure on open road;
very sharp, well-weighted steering; always
stable; handles power very well.

### PERFORMANCE *****
More power is available from the 252 bhp
Boxster S, but the original 2.5 and 2.7
engines are more than adequate; Tiptronic
auto with manual sequential changes is fun
but slows the car down.

### COMFORT ****
Boxster is built for speed, not comfort; very
snug inside with hood raised; not incredibly
quiet and refined; seats are comfortable;
luggage room is limited.

### IMAGE *****
The classic Porsche ingredients – rear-
mounted engine, pretty body; despite its
price tag, it's still a proper Porsche and is
respected and admired as such.

### SAFETY ****
Twin airbags; ABS standard; side airbags
and traction control are costly options; not
as twitchy to drive as Porsches of old.

### SECURITY ****
Superb deadlocks; roof is vulnerable;
immobiliser and alarm are also standard, but
best to fit additional measures.

## Renault Clio (1998-2001)
FOR Space; comfort; value
AGAINST Less fun than the old Clio

### VALUE ****
Well equipped; residual values are now
slipping as the new 'Collection' line-up
devalues 1998-2001 models.

### COSTS ****
Good fuel economy and low insurance; long-
term maintenance costs are lower than the
old model; service intervals have been
stretched to 12-18,000 miles.

### RELIABILITY ****
Solid, chunky Clio feels well made; solidly
constructed body should last well; no
significant problems reported so far.

### DRIVING ****
Easy and relaxing to drive, though not as
nimble and dynamic as its predecessor;
handling is precise and grip is firm; body roll
is well controlled at sensible speeds, though
a bit wobbly if really pushed.

### PERFORMANCE ****
Bodyshell is stronger and heavier than old
Clio, so 1.2 litre has to work hard – it offers
similar performance to 1.9D; 1.4 and 1.6
are quicker and more satisfying; 1.6 16v
versions are lively; 2.0 16v Sport 172 will
please the keenest driver.

### COMFORT ****
Comfy seats; good head- and leg-room;
generous load space; smooth ride and low
noise levels give big-car refinement.

### IMAGE ****
Stylish second generation Clio is classless
yet confidently chic.

### SAFETY ****
Strong body and side impact bars; a high four-star Euro NCAP rating for a 2000 model; passenger airbag optional 1998-2000, standard from 2000 (when side airbag option was introduced); ABS optional where not already standard.

### SECURITY ***
Immobilisers and unique-fit stereos are standard throughout; RXE, Etoile, Initiale and sports models also have an alarm.

## Renault Espace (1991-97)
FOR Excellent cabin
AGAINST Getting on a bit

### VALUE ****
Practical all-rounder that's increasingly affordable; high-spec models preferred – RN is basic by modern standards.

### COSTS ***
Holds its value well; respectable fuel economy from 2.1 TD; frequent minor service intervals.

### RELIABILITY ***
Generally good if looked after, but some older cars can look tatty.

### DRIVING ****
Easy to drive; precise steering; some body roll when cornering; bouncy ride.

### PERFORMANCE ***
2.0 a bit under-powered, gets noisy; V6 is an excellent cruiser but gearing is a bit uneven; TD is less refined but powerful.

### COMFORT ****
Upright driving position; roomy, well designed cabin with adequate load area unless there are seven people on board.

### IMAGE ***
The original article; often imitated but never bettered; ageing but respected.

### SAFETY ***
ABS optional; driver's airbag from 1995.

### SECURITY ***
Immobiliser; alarm on RXE models.

## Renault Megane
FOR Outstanding safety
AGAINST Cramped cabin

### VALUE ****
All models are generously equipped – air conditioning, electric windows and a CD player are standard on most.

### COSTS ****
Good fuel economy — especially the dCi diesels; low insurance groups; long service intervals; depreciation is uncertain.

### RELIABILITY ***
Cabin quality is much improved over the previous model; advanced electronics are similar to the current Laguna, which is not immune to niggling faults.

### DRIVING ****
Good body control and composed handling, spoiled by steering that feels slow-witted and vague; firm ride amplifies bumps; good driving position has plenty of adjustment even for the tallest drivers.

### PERFORMANCE ***
1.4 copes well enough; 1.6 and the 2.0 are better, though all petrol units lack refinement; 1.5 dCi from Clio struggles with the extra weight, but the 1.9 dCi 120 is tolerably refined and torquey.

### COMFORT ***
The rakish roofline and bulbous rear end cut into rear space, with cramped knee- and headroom; legroom at front is OK. Wide, deep boot is compromised by the sloping roof and large rear light clusters.

### IMAGE ***
Striking styling follows Renault's bold design direction. Love-it-or-hate-it looks are controversial but eye-catching.

### SAFETY *****
Performs even better than old Megane, with a best-in-class five-star NCAP crash rating;

driver, passenger, side and curtain airbags, plus standard ABS.

### SECURITY ****
Deadlocks, a Thatcham-approved immobiliser and RAID (Renault Anti-Intruder Device); Privilege also has an alarm.

## Rover 75
FOR Rover refinement and heritage; elegant Tourer estate
AGAINST Mid-range Audi, BMW and Merc models

### VALUE ****
Used prices are falling; not the best-driving or the most prestigious executive contender, but standard equipment is generous; attractive as a used choice.

### COSTS ***
Projected parts and servicing costs are affordable; resale values are better than some experts originally projected, but continuing strength will depend on the good health of MG Rover.

### RELIABILITY ****
Some minor glitches on early cars – should have been ironed out by now; the three-year warranty set a standard which other British car makers rapidly adopted.

### DRIVING ***
Early cars had a rather remote feel, with lifeless steering, a floating ride and some body roll; later cars have been tightened up, but the 75 still falls short of fully satisfying the enthusiastic driver.

### PERFORMANCE ****
Quite a heavy car but it cruises effortlessly; engines are flexible and enjoyably responsive, though power delivery is subtle rather than sporty.

### COMFORT ****
The 75 is smooth, quiet and refined; the retro-styled interior is well designed, classy and soothing; rear legroom is not all that generous for long-legged adults; 'stretch' LWB version is more spacious in the back; roomy boot in the saloon.

### IMAGE ****
Respectable but a bit stuffy; Tourer is a lifestyle choice; 'Connoisseur' badging seems tastelessly self-regarding. A safe corporate choice, but fails to deliver the flair of the Alfa 156 or Jaguar X-Type, the sportier sensibilities of the 3-Series or Lexus IS or the assured competence and solidity of the A4 or Passat.

### SAFETY ****
Front and side airbags; standard ABS and EBD Electronic Brake Distribution system; rear centre three-point seatbelt; strong body helped to achieve a four-star Euro NCAP crash test rating.

### SECURITY ****
Alarm, immobiliser and deadlocks are all standard – protection looks thorough and appears to be effective.

## Vauxhall Corsa (2000 on)
FOR Spacious interior; good looks; refined engines
AGAINST Poor quality trim; tight rear cabin space

### VALUE ****
Well equipped for the money; used prices are already competitive; appears to be well built, although some interior trim is a bit skimpy.

### COSTS ****
Long service intervals, with cheap service and parts costs to attract fleet users; 1.0i and 1.2i petrol engines and the new 1.7 Di and DTi turbo-diesels are particularly frugal; new ECO is a real gallon-stretcher.

### RELIABILITY ****
Previous Corsa was generally reliable; no significant faults reported so far.

### DRIVING ***
Steering is light but let down by a lack of feel and becomes heavy when parking; handling is precise; noticeable body roll when cornering at speed.

### PERFORMANCE ***
1.0 12v is best around town; 1.2 16v needs to be worked quite hard for best results; 1.4 16v and 1.7 DTi are both enjoyably lively; 1.8 16v is the obvious sporting choice but refinement is not its strong point.

### COMFORT ***
Roomier than the old model, although rear space is still at a premium in three-door cars; ride comfort has improved – only big potholes unsettle this Corsa.

### IMAGE ***
Middle-aged supermodel gets a fairly convincing make-over; the result is a car that's fresher and more youthful, but still recognisably a Corsa.

### SAFETY ****
Strong body structure; driver's airbag and active headrests; passenger airbag on Comfort upwards – optional on lesser models; optional side bags; four stars for the NCAP crash test in 2002 puts Corsa alongside the safest superminis.

### SECURITY ****
Immobiliser; deadlocks from Comfort upwards; optional alarm.

## Vauxhall Tigra
FOR Cute styling
AGAINST Uninspiring dynamics; Ford Puma

### VALUE ***
Common, so prices have dropped; Corsa-based design is practical and fun but not really sporty; 1.4 is the best buy.

### COSTS ****
Nearly as cheap to run as equivalent Corsa and holds its value slightly better; sensible insurance and fuel costs.

### RELIABILITY ***
Good if not abused or neglected; build quality not great; some valve problems.

### DRIVING ***
Safe and predictable; more exciting but bumpier than a Corsa; Lotus-tweaked suspension from Oct 1997 livens it up.

### PERFORMANCE ***
Nippy, quite entertaining; not that much difference between 1.4 and costlier 1.6; not particularly refined or smooth.

### COMFORT ***
Supermini practicality; good driving position despite low-slung seats; snug cabin but rear head- and leg-room are minimal for adults; restricted rear vision.

### IMAGE ***
Looks pretty enough but lacks the Puma's sporty edge; credibility has been dented by the far superior Puma.

### SAFETY ****
Driver's airbag; ABS and passenger airbag on 1.6 (options on 1.4).

### SECURITY *****
Deadlocks; micro chip key immobiliser – which appears to be a very effective system.

## Vauxhall Vectra (1995-2002)
FOR Refinement; economy; space; value
AGAINST Indifferent ride and handling

### VALUE ****
Good equipment, and steadily upgraded; lots of ex-fleet cars about, so prices are competitive, especially at car super-markets; basic spec cars are unloved.

### COSTS ***
More complicated than Cavalier, though dealer servicing and parts reasonable; insurance competitive on sub-2.0 litre cars; fuel consumption decent on most.

### RELIABILITY ***
OK on the whole; build quality is variable, affecting paint and trim; some mechanical and electrical/electronics problems; high-milers can show their wear; interiors not that durable.

### DRIVING ***
Happiest and most refined on motorway; less so on twisty roads where handling and ride lack poise and polish; but always safe and predictable; most recent versions with tauter chassis are better.

### PERFORMANCE ****
16-valve 1.8 and 2.0 litre engines are quiet and eager; 1.6 struggles a bit; diesels are unstressed – later DTi engines are preferred; 2.2 and V6 are swift; all cruise happily on the motorway.

### COMFORT ***
Decent cabin space; good driving position and visibility; big boot; estate is not as spacious as some rivals; not much standard equipment on base models – go for Club, LS or higher.

### IMAGE ***
Competent and comfortable but never covetable; fleet favourite or flexible family friend; a sensible cost-efficient choice rather than a status symbol.

### SAFETY ****
Rates three stars for Euro NCAP crash test; ABS on all models; driver's airbag, plus passenger airbag on newer cars; side airbags optional since 1997 and standard from October 2000.

### SECURITY ****
Vauxhall's superb deadlocks, linked to an effective immobiliser system, do a very good job.

## Volkswagen Golf (1992-98)
FOR Quality, reputation; reliability
AGAINST Little chance of finding a bargain

### VALUE ****
Superior prices for superior cars; few rivals can match Golf's longevity.

### COSTS ***
Reasonable fuel economy (excellent from TDi); insurance average; long service intervals but some parts expensive.

### RELIABILITY ****
Few problems if servicing is carried out as stipulated; GTi 16v and VR6 tend to be driven hard and suffer if neglected.

### DRIVING ****
Superbly balanced handling, excellent grip and precise though weighty steering; parking is heavy work without PAS.

### PERFORMANCE ***
Heavy body; 1.4 is underpowered; GTi is slower than many rivals, though 16v and VR6 have power in reserve.

### COMFORT ****
Tasteful but sombre cabin; good seats; generous rear accommodation and load space; ride is firm but acceptable.

### IMAGE ***
Dependable and still desirable; cast iron reputation upholds conservative values; GTi isn't quite the icon it once was.

### SAFETY ***
Sturdy body offers good protection, but this Golf is too old for NCAP test; ABS optional across the range, standard on later sports models; airbag from 1994.

### SECURITY ***
Early locks are not good – but better on later cars; immobiliser from late 1994.

## Volvo S40, V40
FOR Wide choice of specs; safe; refined; comfortable
AGAINST Could be more engaging to drive

### VALUE ***
Used prices are easing, particularly for first generation 1996-2000 cars; there are lots of fairly low-spec ex-fleet cars about – these are much less desirable than fully loaded cars; option packs add to appeal but can be confusing and are often difficult to value.

### COSTS ***
Running costs are lower than big Volvos, but still not cheap; wholly dependent on dealer network for parts and servicing; resale values are only average, with base models depreciating the fastest.

### RELIABILITY ***
Some build quality niggles on 1996-97 cars but overall a big improvement on the old 400 series; reliability on newer cars is above

average, but look for full Volvo history for peace of mind.

### DRIVING ***

Responses are refined but not very involving; early cars suffered from a very firm ride; 2.0T and T4 models are more dynamic though still feel slightly remote; the chassis allows safe, predictable handling and imparts confidence to the driver, but it could be more refined.

### PERFORMANCE ***

1.6 is a shade underpowered; 1.9 turbo-diesel is workmanlike; 1.8 and 2.0 are adequate; 2.0T is enjoyably swift; T4 turbo is simply manic – but fun.

### COMFORT ***

Spacious interior; supportive seats; safe, sophisticated ambience; S40's boot is fine, but V40 estate is not that spacious.

### IMAGE ****

Mid-market appeal combines safety with a dash of style in a civilised package – it's almost a compact executive range; top-end Turbo models help to shrug off Volvo's staid old image; V40 2.0T or T4 are quite fashionable 'lifestyle' choices.

### SAFETY ****

Four stars in Euro NCAP crash test; excellent side impact protection system; seat belt pre-tensioners, ABS on all models.

### SECURITY ****

Immobiliser standard; deadlocks on all but base models (where it's an option with remote central locking).

# Index

# Acknowledgements

Many who work in the motor industry (some in senior positions) admit in private that things need to change in the way it operates.

I am grateful to those wanting to see improvements who trusted me with confidences, and enabled me to write a book that I hope will contribute to a more open and honest relationship between those who build/sell cars and those who buy them. The experiences of many motorists, as told to me, were valuable in identifying issues that cause anxiety. The book includes lists, data and other material from a wide range of sources selected with the intention of giving consumers the opportunity to buy with more confidence. Websites with information helping to demystify the process of car purchase are listed in the book.

Material from the industry, other organisations and magazines is published with an acknowledgement of the source. I especially appreciate the agreement of Car magazine and Parker's used & new car Chooser to agree to the inclusion of an evaluation of cars.